ANTHROPOLOGICAL PAPERS OF
THE UNIVERSITY OF ARIZONA
NUMBER 72

Ancestral Zuni Glaze-Decorated Pottery

Viewing Pueblo IV Regional Organization through Ceramic Production and Exchange

Deborah L. Huntley

THE UNIVERSITY OF ARIZONA PRESS
TUCSON
2008

About the author

DEBORAH L. HUNTLEY completed her undergraduate studies in Anthropology at the University of Colorado, graduating in 1991. She received her Master's degree in 1995 (in Anthropology and Museum Studies) and her Doctoral degree in Anthropology in 2004, both from Arizona State University in Tempe. Her expertise is primarily in Southwestern prehistory, particularly ceramic studies; additionally, she has participated in a wide variety of archaeological research projects in Arizona, New Mexico, southern California, and Germany. Dr. Huntley was a teaching assistant for several Arizona State University archaeological field schools and in 1998 co-directed an ASU field school (with Suzanne Eckert) near Albuquerque, New Mexico. She has taught at Arizona and New Mexico community colleges and from 2005–2007 was appointed to the Adjunct Faculty at the University of New Mexico. From 2004–2007, Dr. Huntley served as a Project Director for Southwest Archaeological Consultants, Inc., in Santa Fe, New Mexico. She was appointed a Preservation Archaeologist at the Center for Desert Archaeology in Tucson, Arizona in 2007.

Cover: Ancestral Zuni glaze-decorated bowls in the collections of the Arizona State Museum. *Left to right*: Kwakina Polychrome, Heshotauthla Polychrome, and St. Johns Polychrome (see p. xi for rim diameters). Photograph by Jannelle Weakly, Photographer at the Arizona State Museum, University of Arizona, Tucson.

THE UNIVERSITY OF ARIZONA PRESS
Copyright © 2008
The Arizona Board of Regents
All Rights Reserved

This book was set in 11/12 Times New Roman.
Manufactured in the United States of America on acid-free, archival-quality paper containing a minimum of 30% post-consumer waste and processed chlorine free.

Library of Congress Cataloging-in-Publication Data

Huntley, Deborah L., 1969–
   Ancestral Zuni glaze-decorated pottery : viewing
Pueblo IV regional organization through ceramic
production and exchange / Deborah L. Huntley.
      p. cm. — (Anthropological papers of the
University of Arizona ; no. 72)
   Includes bibliographical references and index.
   ISBN 978-0-8165-2564-5 (pbk. : alk. paper)
   1. Pottery—Themes, motives. 2. Pottery—Analysis.
3. Glazes—Southwest, New. 4. Glazing (Ceramics)
5. Southwest, New—Antiquities. I. Title.
E99.Z9H86 2008
738.1'44—dc22   2007041151

For Jim and Sean

Contents

FIGURES

TABLES

Preface

Material culture, notably pottery, is in many ways the currency of social transactions. Prehistorically, ceramic containers played a key role in the creation and maintenance of social identity, the definition of social group boundaries, and the negotiation of social relationships through exchange. One problem for archaeologists interested in understanding interaction and identity is that both social theory and ethnographic research indicate these variables are situational and mutable. At issue is the extent to which boundaries and connections among social groups are typically visible to archaeologists, and, if so, what they actual signify. One way to begin to investigate social group affiliation is to examine interactions at different spatial and temporal scales using multiple lines of evidence.

Across the northern southwestern United States, the Pueblo IV period (A.D. 1275–1600 following Adams and Duff 2004) was a time of dramatic change in settlement patterns and religious configurations. During the A.D. 1275 to 1400 interval, local populations in the Zuni region of west-central New Mexico combined and recombined into a series of nucleated pueblos that were clustered across the landscape. This pattern is not only the hallmark of the thirteenth and fourteenth century Zuni region, but also of much of the northern Southwest. During this time of social transformation, individuals renegotiated their social boundaries, redefined their social identities, and reestablished their social connections.

In the Zuni region, there are three primary scales at which individuals focused social interactions and defined social group membership: within spatially clustered groups of pueblos, among different pueblo clusters, and with other regions. To explore these scales I analyzed the production and exchange of polychrome and utility ware vessels, aspects of glaze paint technology and design styles shared by Zuni region potters, and the utilization of raw materials for glaze paint manufacture. The resulting multiscalar perspective on early Pueblo IV Zuni regional organization reveals that social group membership was defined through participation in overlapping spheres of interaction with permeable and flexible boundaries. Zuni region potters, as well as other individuals with access to the products of potters, used ceramic vessels to negotiate relationships within these overlapping spheres of interaction.

For this research I used ceramic assemblages from nine nucleated pueblos: four located in the El Morro Valley in the eastern portion of the Zuni region (Pueblo de los Muertos, Atsinna, Cienega, and Mirabal), two located in the central part of the Zuni region along the Rio Pescado (Heshotauthla Pueblo and Lower Pescado Village), one located in the northern portion of the Zuni region (Box S Pueblo), and two located along Jaralosa Draw in the southwestern Zuni region (Spier 170 and Ojo Bonito). All nine pueblos were occupied during all or part of the early Pueblo IV period (A.D. 1275–1400).

I relied exclusively on existing archaeological collections for this study. Excavations were conducted at the El Morro Valley pueblos in 1972 and 1973 as part of the Cibola Archaeological Research Project (CARP) directed by Patty Jo Watson, Charles Redman, and Steven LeBlanc. Keith Kintigh directed the Heshotauthla Archaeological Research Project (HARP) as part of an Arizona State University (ASU) field school in 1990 and 1991. Kintigh also directed a mapping project at Box S Pueblo in 1997 designed to document the extent of looting at this site and controlled surface collections were made at this time. Excavations at Lower Pescado Village were conducted by Nan Rothschild and Susan Dublin in 1990 as part of the Columbia University/Barnard College Archaeological Field School (Rothschild and Dublin 1995). Ceramics from Ojo Bonito and Spier 170 came from limited test excavations and surface collections conducted by Arizona State University in 1987 and 1994, and from samples collected by Duff (1999, 2002) as part of his dissertation research.

To begin, I review Zuni region culture history and settlement patterns with particular attention to the

[ix]

organizational parameters of nucleated pueblos, spatial patterning and occupational histories of nucleated pueblo clusters, and regional population movement (Chapter 1). In Chapter 2, after reviewing some basic principles of production, exchange, and interaction in middle-range societies, like those in the Pueblo IV period American Southwest, I develop expectations for identifying aspects of social interaction using various analyses presented in subsequent chapters. Building on previous studies of Zuni glaze-decorated pottery, Chapter 3 focuses on identifying ceramic production loci and tracking ceramic circulation using Instrumental Neutron Activation Analysis (INAA). Chapter 4 details electron microprobe analysis of glaze compositions and identified glaze recipes. Long-distance interaction is highlighted by lead isotope analysis of lead ore sources used by Zuni region potters (Chapter 5). The concluding chapter provides a multiscalar perspective on Zuni regional organization supported by multiple lines of evidence. This research shows that organizational scenarios applied to other areas of the American Southwest do not fully capture the complex nature of Pueblo IV Zuni regional social dynamics and demonstrates the long-term research potential of historic collections.

Acknowledgments

Many institutions and individuals have supported this research. Funding for electron microprobe and High Resolution Magnetic Sector Inductively-Coupled Plasma Mass Spectrometry (Hr ICP-MS) analyses was provided by the National Science Foundation (Grant Number BCS–0003191), by the Wenner-Gren Foundation for Anthropological Research (Grant Number 6659), and by a Fred Plog Fellowship I received from the Society for American Archaeology. The INAA study was further supported by the Archaeometry Program at the Research Reactor Center, University of Missouri, Columbia (NSF Grant Number SBR–9802366), under the direction of Michael Glascock and Hector Neff. Jeff Speakman and Kyra Lienhop performed the lab work for the analysis. I thank Dr. Neff in particular for his thorough statistical analysis and coherent interpretation of an especially complicated dataset. The Center for Desert Archaeology, Tucson, generously subsidized publication costs, and the Department of Anthropology at the University of Arizona, courtesy of John W. Olsen, Head, kindly supplied funds for the color cover.

The following individuals generously granted me access to their collections or allowed me to use their data: Susan Dublin, Andrew Duff, Keith Kintigh, Steven LeBlanc, Barbara Mills, Charles Redman, Nan Rothschild, and Patty Jo Watson. Their work and my own research would have been impossible without the long-standing cooperation and support of the people of the Pueblo of Zuni. I am also indebted to Homer Milford, formerly of the State of New Mexico Mining and Minerals Division, Santa Fe, and Robert Weber, Emeritus, of the New Mexico Bureau of Geology and Mineral Resources, Socorro, for tracking down ores for lead isotope analysis and for answering my many geology questions. Special thanks go to Elizabeth Monroe and Jenna Hamlin for their gracious hospitality while I was visiting collections at Washington University. I am particularly grateful to Keith Kintigh, Katherine Spielmann, and Barbara Stark. Each brought to bear his or her unique perspective on this research, and each has influenced the final product in significant ways.

I conducted an electron microprobe pilot study in the Department of Geology at ASU with the helpful technical assistance of the late James Clark. Subsequent microprobe and lead isotope analyses were conducted on equipment available in the Earth and Marine Sciences facilities at the University of California, Santa Cruz. A number of UCSC students, faculty, and staff generously donated their time, expertise, and support to ensure the success of this project: Ryan Dean, Russ Flegal, Rob Franks, Diane Gifford-Gonzales, Jon Krupp, Mara Ranville, Dan Sampson, Bruce Tanner, and especially Judith Habicht-Mauche.

I am most appreciative of the efforts of Allyson Carter of the University of Arizona Press and Carol Gifford, Editor of the *Anthropological Papers* for their interest in this research and for enthusiastically shepherding this manuscript through the publication process. I would also like to thank Barbara Mills for her support of this research and its publication. Thoughtful critiques by three anonymous reviewers have much improved the content of this manuscript, although I alone am responsible for any errors or omissions therein.

At the University of Arizona, María Nieves Zedeño, Bureau of Applied Research, kindly translated the Abstract into Spanish. Also especially appreciated is the technical assistance of Dirk J. Harris, Desktop Services Manager in the College of Social and Behavioral Sciences, and David C. Thompsen, Support Systems Analyst in the Department of Anthropology. At the

Arizona State Museum, Tucson, G. Michael Jacobs, Curatorial Museum Specialist, was particularly helpful in finding suitable nonfunerary vessels for the cover illustration, which was taken by Jannelle Weakly, the Museum photographer. Also of notable value have been the supporting services of Patrick D. Lyons, Associate Curator of Collections.

Many of my friends and colleagues provided valuable moral support and intellectual stimulation during the course of this research. Special thanks go to Sherri Andrews, Tiffany Clark, Linda Cordell, Andrew Duff, Suzanne (SuS) Eckert, Donna Glowacki, Billy Graves, Judith Habicht-Mauche, Cynthia Herhahn, Brett Hill, Jim Potter, Melissa Powell, Greg Schachner, Cherie Scheick, Mark Varien, and Christian Wells. SuS deserves particular recognition. I never would have made it through this process without her friendship and special ability to put things into perspective. Most of all, thanks go to all of my family members for their enduring confidence and support.

Deborah L. Huntley
May 2007

[Editor's note: Special acknowledgment is expressed to María Nieves Zedeño for her continued service. She has translated the Abstract into Spanish for nearly a dozen *Anthropological Papers*, including No. 71, and her prompt attention is always appreciated. The on-going technical assistance of Dirk J. Harris, Desktop Services Manager in the College of Social and Behavioral Sciences, and David C. Thompsen, Support Systems Analyst in the Department of Anthropology also merits special attention. Digital production of the *Papers* would not be possible without their intelligence, wit, creativity, and patience, which were especially necessary and relied on for the production of *Paper* No. 71. Additionally, Wm. Randy Haas, Jr., IGERT Fellow in the Department of Anthropology, University of Arizona, provided significant assistance with the production of PDF files for *Paper* No. 72.

Carol A. Gifford
May 2007]

Illustrations

The Museum of Indian Arts and Culture/Laboratory of Anthropology (www.miaclab.org) in Santa Fe, New Mexico, granted permission to publish the vessel images in Figures 2.1–2.3 and 2.6–2.8. The photographs were taken by Deborah L. Huntley.

Figs. 2.1, 2.2: St. Johns Polychrome bowl (08872/11)
Fig. 2.3:   St. Johns Polychrome bowl (46361/11)
Fig. 2.6:   Kwakina Polychrome bowl (54235/11)
Figs. 2.7, 2.8: Kwakina Polychrome bowl (20980/11)

The images of Heshotauthla Polychrome bowls in Figures 2.4 (no catalogue no.) and 2.5 (PM 108–06) are printed courtesy of the Cibola Archaeological Research Project with permission of co-director Patty Jo Watson, Edward Mallinckrodt Distinguished University Professor Emerita, Washington University, St. Louis, Missouri.

The Arizona State Museum, University of Arizona, Tucson, granted permission to publish the vessel images appearing on the cover. The bowls were photographed by Jannelle Weakly, Photographer at the Arizona State Museum.

Left to right:
  Kwakina Polychrome bowl
    (ASM 23823; rim diameter 27 cm)
  Heshotauthla Polychrome bowl
    (ASM 87–26–2; rim diameter 27 cm)
  St. Johns Polychrome bowl
    (GP2985; rim diameter 21.5 cm)

CHAPTER ONE

The Pueblo IV Zuni Region

Throughout the history of North American archaeology, researchers have conceived of regions as spatial units of analysis. The American Southwest is no exception, and our current regional concepts are deeply rooted in the culture area concept (Duff 2000; Neitzel 2000). Although the region as a unit of analysis is expedient when delineating spatial and temporal components for archaeological investigations, at issue is the scale at which individuals within archaeologically defined regions focused their social interactions and conceived of their social identities. I am not the first to argue that the concept of region is too large and abstract to have been a meaningful entity to people on a daily basis and that smaller scale organizational units operated within regions (Bernardini 2002, 2005; Mills 2007; see also Neitzel 1999; Hegmon 2000). These organizational units included, among other things, the individual nucleated pueblo, complementary pairs of pueblos, and clustered groups of pueblos within regions. There must also have been internal subdivisions within pueblos based on gender, households, kinship, ritual societies, or other social groups, but these kinds of subdivisions are much more difficult to detect archaeologically.

The Zuni region (Fig. 1.1), the focus of this volume, is part of the larger Cibola cultural area of east-central Arizona and west-central New Mexico. It includes some 4,800 square kilometers (1,853 square miles) of the Zuni River drainage, all of the present-day Zuni Reservation, the El Morro Valley to the east of the reservation, and Jaralosa Draw, located south of the reservation boundary (Duff 2000; Kintigh 1996). I include Jaralosa Draw within the traditional boundaries of the Zuni region (Kintigh 1996: 132) even though this area may also have had close ties with the Upper Little Colorado area (Duff 1999, 2002). Pueblos in the El Morro Valley likely also had ties to Ácoma, with which Zuni shared a ceramic tradition (Dittert 1998).

During the Pueblo IV period, defined in this volume following Adams and Duff (2004: 3) as A.D. 1275–1600, the archaeological record suggests that there were fundamental shifts in the scales at which social group membership was defined. Although many parts of the northern Southwest were abandoned, large populations in other areas became concentrated in single, apartment-like structures called nucleated pueblos. In the Zuni region and elsewhere in the Western Pueblo area, nucleated pueblos often were clustered across the landscape and shared similarities in material culture, particularly decorated pottery (Duff 2000; Upham 1982). This phenomenon has led a number of researchers to propose the development of multipueblo sociopolitical integration at the level of pueblo clusters (LeBlanc 1989, 2000; Upham 1982). Some researchers focus on interactions within nucleated pueblos and relatively strong intrapueblo integration as primary structuring principles in Pueblo IV social life (Bernardini 1998; Reid and Whittlesey 1999); others postulate regional integration via centralized political systems (Upham 1982; Upham and Reed 1989). Situated between these extremes are various scholars who surmise some degree of regional sociopolitical integration in the absence of centralized authority. Such integration may have taken the form of informal, periodic suprapueblo entities (Habicht-Mauche 1993; Spielmann 1994), alliances among equal polities (LeBlanc 1989, 2000), decision-making hierarchies (Lightfoot and Upham 1989; F. Plog 1985; F. Plog and Upham 1983; Stone 1992; Upham and F. Plog 1986; Wilcox 1991), or complementary relationships between pueblo pairs (Potter 1997; Potter and Perry 2000).

The term pueblo herein refers to a block of contiguous rooms used mainly for permanent habitation. Ranging widely in size, the pueblo was the basic building block for residential settlements in the Zuni region and across the northern Southwest after about A.D. 1000. The nucleated pueblo is a distinctive Pueblo IV phenomenon incorporating multiple, contiguous room blocks into a single, apartmentlike structure. Contemporaneous nucleated pueblos often form spatially distinct clusters, or groups, with unoccupied areas between clusters. I

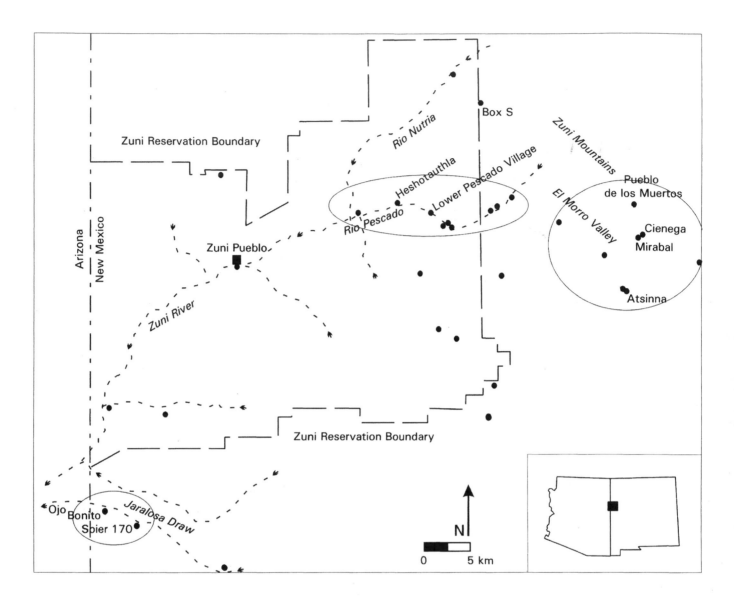

Figure 1.1. Pueblo IV sites (dots) in the Zuni region with sampled
pueblos identified; circles enclose pueblo clusters.

generally reserve the term village or town (except where
the term is part of a proper name, as in the case of
Lower Pescado Village) for non-nucleated pueblos with
separate room blocks in close proximity (that is, aggregated), much like the present-day Pueblo of Zuni. I use
the term community not only in the sense of an identifiable residential group, but also in the sense of multiple
residential groups linked by political, economic, and
social ties (Wills and Leonard 1994: xiii–xv). This
flexible definition means that communities may be
identified at multiple scales.

ZUNI REGION CHRONOLOGY AND SETTLEMENT PATTERNS

Because the traditional Pecos classification (Kidder
1924) typically is not applied to the Zuni region (indeed,
its use is somewhat problematic for much of the ancestral Pueblo Southwest; Adams and Duff 2004: 3–5), an
explanation of the chronology used throughout this
monograph is necessary. Prior to about A.D. 1150 in the
Zuni region, the Pecos classification of Basketmaker II
through Pueblo II/Chaco era is generally accepted.

However, the period A.D. 1150–1275, which falls within the Pecos Pueblo III period, is now termed the post-Chaco era (Fowler and Stein 1992; Kintigh 1994, 1996; Kintigh and others 1996). The appearance of nucleated pueblos in the Zuni region (and elsewhere) around A.D. 1275 marks the transition to the Pueblo IV period.

Recent research indicates the Pueblo IV period can be subdivided into three phases: A.D. 1275–1325, 1325–1400, and 1400–1600 (see also Adams 2002; Adams and Duff 2004; Duff 2000, 2002; Mills and Herr 1999). Across much of the Western Pueblo world, these intervals correspond with changes in ceramic design and technology, as well as shifts in settlement patterns and architectural layouts (Adams and Duff 2004: 3–4). Throughout this volume I use the term early Pueblo IV for the time period A.D. 1275–1325 and late Pueblo IV for the time period A.D. 1325–1400, recognizing that these subdivisions are specific to portions of the Western Pueblo area, including the Zuni region. Because the third interval, A.D. 1400–1600, is marked by a major shift in Zuni region settlement organization and many pueblos founded during this interval continued to be occupied into the historic period, I refer to this interval as protohistoric (Huntley and Kintigh 2004; Kintigh 1990, 2000).

According to Duff (2002: 43), the Zuni region conforms to traditional notions of the "ideal" region based on its consistent developmental history, its stable and high population levels during a long period of time compared to surrounding regions, and its distinctive material culture assemblage. Nevertheless, regional patterns of settlement organization changed dramatically through time and scales of interactions presumably did as well.

Between A.D. 1000 and 1150, corresponding with the late Chaco period, much of the Zuni region population lived in pueblos of 10 to 20 rooms (Kintigh 1985a, 2007). The larger room blocks often had an associated subterranean kiva. Some room blocks were dispersed and others were loosely clustered in what appear to have been communities (Kintigh and others 2004), the largest of which had more than 150 rooms, although probably not all rooms were simultaneously occupied. During the post-Chacoan period (A.D. 1150–1250), larger aggregated villages of 500 rooms or more in multiple room blocks were constructed (Kintigh and others 1996). Post-Chacoan communities in the Zuni region were often focused around great houses and oversized, apparently unroofed, great kivas (Duff 1993; Eckert

1995; Huntley and Schachner 1999; Kintigh and others 1996; Schachner 2007).

Beginning around A.D. 1250 at the Pueblo III to Pueblo IV transition (Potter 1997), patterns of community organization in the Zuni region changed dramatically with the construction of the first nucleated pueblos (Duff 2000; Kintigh 1985a; LeBlanc 2001; Schachner 2007). Much of what we know about Pueblo IV settlement patterns is based on previous seriations of ceramic assemblages from several archaeological surveys and excavations (Kintigh 1985a; Spier 1917; Watson and others 1980). Fortunately, the relative abundances of different Pueblo IV pottery types made in the Zuni region changed rapidly and these pottery types are reasonably well cross-dated using stratigraphic associations and tree-ring dates (Chapter 2). Available data indicate that 41 large, nucleated pueblos were built in the Zuni region between A.D. 1250 and 1540 (Huntley and Kintigh 2004). By A.D. 1300 at the latest, the entire Zuni-area population apparently resided in nucleated pueblos.

Nucleated pueblos are distinguished from earlier large, aggregated villages in that the former typically consisted of a single block of contiguous rooms (between 200 and 1,200 total) surrounding a central plaza (Kintigh 1985a; Spier 1917). Most nucleated pueblos clearly were planned and appear to have been built during a short period of time, although some rooms were often added later (Anyon 1987; Duff 2000, 2002; Kintigh 1985a; Watson and others 1980). In the Zuni region, nucleated pueblos were constructed in a limited number of architectural forms: either generally rectangular or oval. Some of the earliest Pueblo IV nucleated pueblos were irregular and a few had a composite oval and rectangular shape (Kintigh 1985a). Huntley and Kintigh (2004) argue that the oval and rectangular architectural configurations were contemporaneous and that the different shapes must have been socially meaningful. One interpretation, advanced by Potter (1997; Potter and Perry 2000), is that Pueblo IV Zuni cosmology was embodied in the ritual interdependence of rectangular-shaped and oval-shaped nucleated pueblos.

Notably, nucleated pueblos were initially formed by the coalescence of populations that had previously lived in aggregated communities. Many aggregated communities likely incorporated groups that were similar in size to the populations of nucleated pueblos, but, significantly, their layouts, which consisted of multiple room blocks, afforded some degree of physical and social separation among neighbors. During the Pueblo IV period, relative strangers suddenly found themselves sharing walls within the highly structured and consolidated spaces of nucleated pueblos.

There were both dramatic and subtle changes in Zuni region settlement patterns during the Pueblo IV period. Huntley and Kintigh (2004) identify two to three groups of spatially clustered pueblos and several isolated pueblos. Although the locations and configurations of pueblo clusters varied through time, they were typically between 8 km and 10 km (5–6.2 miles) across, were separated from each other by 16 km to 20 km (10–12.4 miles), and contained between three and five pueblos each. Figure 1.1 shows the locations of all known Pueblo IV nucleated pueblos within the Zuni region. Sites discussed in detail are labeled, as are pueblo clusters. It is unlikely that additional large pueblos remain to be discovered within the region. Since Spier's (1917) survey, only one new nucleated pueblo, Pescado Canyon, has been reported.

Early Pueblo IV nucleated pueblos (A.D. 1275–1325) were consistently located at higher elevations (more than 2,013 m; 6,600 feet) compared with late Pueblo IV period (A.D. 1325–1400) pueblos and in a wider variety of topographic locations, including mesa tops and canyon floors (Kintigh 1985a). Both rectangular and oval pueblos were common, and at least two pueblos had a composite layout including oval and rectangular components. During the early Pueblo IV period, a large concentration of eight nucleated pueblos was situated in the El Morro Valley. Other early Pueblo IV settlements were located along the Pescado, Nutria, and Zuni rivers, in the vicinity of the southeastern portion of the modern Zuni Indian Reservation, and along Jaralosa Draw.

During the late Pueblo IV period, several new nucleated pueblos were built and some founded during the early Pueblo IV period were no longer occupied or had reduced populations (Duff 2000; Kintigh 1985a). Many fewer nucleated pueblos overall were occupied during the late Pueblo IV period and there were none with a thousand rooms or more. With the exception of Lower Pescado Village, which probably housed a small number of people into the fifteenth century (Rothschild and Dublin 1995) and Halona:wa North (Zuni Pueblo), all of the large Pueblo IV nucleated pueblos in the Zuni region were unoccupied by the late 1300s.

Spatial clustering of nucleated pueblos during the late Pueblo IV period is even more obvious than during the preceding early Pueblo IV period. During the late Pueblo IV interval the El Morro Valley cluster contained three pueblos (Pueblo de los Muertos, Cienega, and Atsinna) and the Pescado Springs cluster contained five pueblos (Heshotauthla; Lower Pescado Village; and West, Lower, and Upper Pescado ruins). An additional isolated pair of pueblos (perhaps representing a cluster) was located in Jaralosa Draw. Late Pueblo IV period clusters were around 10 km (6.2 miles) across and were separated from other clusters by at least 20 km (12.4 miles). Intracluster pueblo spacing also changed from a few hundred meters, on average, during the early Pueblo IV period to a few kilometers in the late Pueblo IV period, although late Pueblo IV Pescado Springs and Pescado West are only about a hundred meters apart.

In addition to spatial clustering of nucleated pueblos, there are indications that regional variability in demography and settlement patterns may have persisted over a long time. For example, the eastern portion of the Zuni region was more densely populated throughout the Pueblo IV period than the region's western and southern portions (Kintigh 1996; Kintigh and others 2004; Watson and others 1980). Furthermore, the residents of Heshotauthla Pueblo apparently had a longer history in the immediate area (although with significant population in-migration) than did inhabitants of the El Morro Valley, Box S Pueblo, or Lower Pescado Village. Full-coverage survey of 10.4 square kilometers (4 square miles) surrounding Heshotauthla Pueblo indicates the presence of small-scale settlement clusters in this area as early as A.D. 900 (Kintigh and others 2004: 41). Local populations apparently coalesced into the pueblo of Heshotauthla around A.D. 1275.

The El Morro Valley, in contrast, was sparsely populated before about A.D. 1225, when immigrants to the region constructed the aggregated Scribe S community, a village of clustered room blocks (Kintigh 1985a; Kintigh and others 2004; LeBlanc 2000; Watson and others 1980). The Scribe S inhabitants apparently also built and occupied the planned, nucleated pueblo of Pueblo de los Muertos around the same time that Heshotauthla Pueblo was constructed. Systematic survey is lacking for the areas surrounding Lower Pescado Village and Box S Pueblo, but there is little evidence of substantial population in the vicinity of Box S prior to A.D. 1250 and prior to A.D. 1300 near Lower Pescado Village (Kintigh 1985a, 1996, Appendix).

Another major shift in settlement locations occurred with the onset of the protohistoric period. Beginning around A.D. 1400, the eastern and southernmost portions

Table 1.1. Characteristics of Sampled Zuni Sites

Site	Location	Layout	No. of Rooms	Occupation Dates	Dating Method
Pueblo de los Muertos	El Morro Valley	Rectangular	880	A.D. 1275–1375	Tree-rings; ceramic seriation
Atsinna	El Morro Valley	Rectangular	875	A.D. 1275–1385	Tree-rings; ceramic seriation
Cienega	El Morro Valley	Oval	500	A.D. 1275–1375	Tree-rings; ceramic seriation
Mirabal	El Morro Valley	Oval	740	A.D. 1275–1325	Tree-rings; ceramic seriation
Heshotauthla	Pescado Basin	Oval (?)	875	A.D. 1275–1385	Tree-rings; ceramic seriation
Lower Pescado Village	Pescado Basin	Oval (?)	420 (?)	A.D. 1300–1400*	Ceramic seriation
Box S Pueblo	North-central Zuni region	Rectangular	1000 +	A.D. 1225–1290	Ceramic seriation
Ojo Bonito	Southwest Zuni region	Rectangular	225	A.D. 1300–1385	Ceramic seriation
Spier 170	Southwest Zuni region	Trapezoidal	200	A.D. 1300–1385	Ceramic seriation

NOTE: Data compiled by Huntley and Kintigh (2004, Appendix).

*There may have been an earlier occupation that was not sampled.

of the Zuni region were abandoned and the entire regional population became concentrated into nine villages, many of which were occupied into the historic period (Kintigh 1985a, 1996; Watson and others 1980). Nucleated pueblos were replaced by similarly sized settlements that generally had multiple room blocks and plazas.

Protohistoric villages often appear unplanned compared with earlier nucleated pueblos, and their final complex architectural configurations may be the result of a long period of accretional growth. Kintigh (2000) provides evidence for inequality in religious and political authority among these towns and argues that inter-village variability in mortuary goods reflects social and political boundary maintenance, possibly even ethnic differences, among them. Such ethnic differences may have had their origin in the demographic reorganization of the preceding early and late Pueblo IV periods.

There are a number of possible reasons why population movement was so pervasive during the Pueblo IV period. The simplest explanation is the need to find suitable marriage partners, because it is unlikely that nucleated pueblos could have been entirely endogamous. Social stress and factionalism may have been major reasons for people to move. In fact, Duff (2002) attributes the complete abandonment of many nucleated pueblos to factionalism. Most nucleated pueblos, although they were clearly the result of a planned design and substantial labor investment, were nevertheless occupied only for a few generations (Duff 2000).

As some pueblos were abandoned and others were founded during the course of the Pueblo IV period, populations were again reshuffled. There is no reason to assume that such movement involved the wholesale relocation of the residents of individual nucleated pueblos. It seems more likely, as first suggested by Kintigh (1985a), that the shifting locations of nucleated pueblos within the Pueblo IV Zuni region were the result of the combining and recombining of various social groups, each bringing with them preexisting social connections. These preexisting connections, along with social pressures resulting from regular population movement and regional demographic variability, probably introduced an element of instability into everyday social discourse that resulted in the constant renegotiation of social relationships.

DESCRIPTIONS OF SAMPLED PUEBLOS

I sampled ceramic assemblages from nine Pueblo IV period nucleated pueblos in the Zuni region (Table 1.1). Of these, four are located in the El Morro Valley in the eastern Zuni region (Pueblo de los Muertos, Atsinna, Cienega, and Mirabal), two are located in the central Zuni region along the Rio Pescado (Heshotauthla Pueblo and Lower Pescado Village), one is located in the northern Zuni region (Box S Pueblo), and two are located along Jaralosa Draw in the southwest Zuni region (Spier 170 and Ojo Bonito; Fig. 1.1). A distance of approximately 25 km (15.5 miles) separates Hesho-

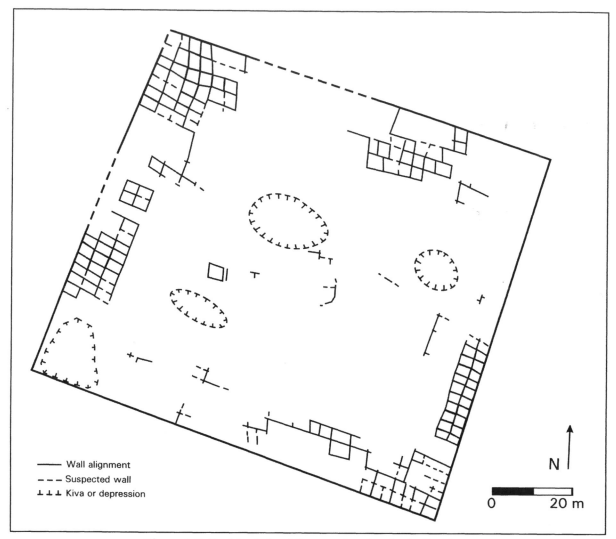

Figure 1.2. Pueblo de los Muertos site plan (redrafted from
Kintigh 1985a, Fig. 4.32; Watson and others 1980, Fig. 4).

tauthla and Lower Pescado Village from the El Morro
Valley pueblos. Box S Pueblo is located approximately
15 km (9.3 miles) northeast of Lower Pescado Village.
Ojo Bonito and Spier 170 are located more than 50 km
(31 miles) from Heshotauthla in the far southwestern
periphery of the Zuni region. I selected these pueblos
because they had roughly contemporaneous occupations
during the Pueblo IV period (Table 1.1) and because
most have accessible ceramic collections from excavated
contexts (a few have surface collections only). Because
our knowledge of many of these pueblos has changed
somewhat since Kintigh's (1985a) study, I provide a
brief description and plan view for each pueblo and
include a history of archaeological investigations and
summary of available occupation dates. Pueblo chronol-

ogies are based on tree-ring dates (where available) and
ceramic cross-dating.

Pueblo de los Muertos

Pueblo de los Muertos (Fig. 1.2; LA1585; CS 139) is
one of several large, nucleated pueblos located in the El
Morro Valley (Fig. 1.1). The available archaeological
evidence suggests that the pueblo was constructed
according to a preconceived plan with later additions
(Watson and others 1980). Pueblo de los Muertos is
rectangular in shape and consists of three to four rows of
rooms on each side of an open plaza (Fig. 1.2). The
inner rows of rooms are built over plaza trash and thus
appear to have been added some time after the pueblo's

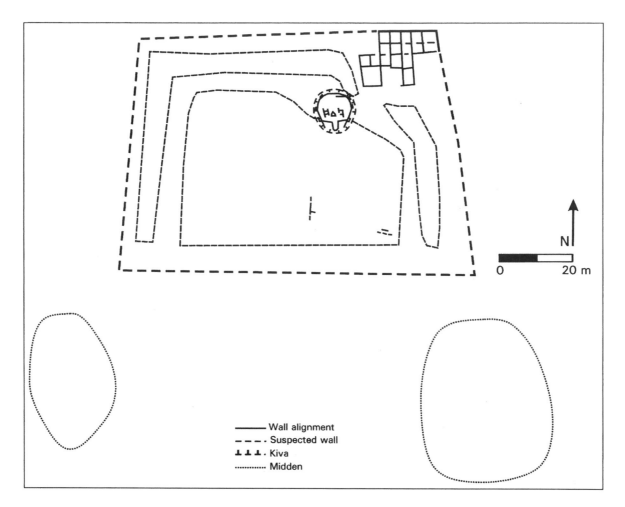

Figure 1.3. Atsinna Pueblo site plan (redrafted from Kintigh 1985, Fig. 4.33; Watson and others 1980, Fig. 7).

initial construction. The pueblo contained nearly 900 rooms by its final occupation (Huntley and Kintigh 2004, Appendix; Kintigh 1985a: 51).

Excavations were conducted at Pueblo de los Muertos in 1972 and 1973 as part of the Cibola Archaeological Research Project (CARP) directed by Patty Jo Watson, Charles Redman, and Steven LeBlanc. CARP excavated 15 trash-filled rooms and several trenches in the plaza and outside the pueblo's exterior wall (Watson and others 1980). Tree-ring dates from Pueblo de los Muertos cluster between A.D. 1260 and 1290, including a cutting date of A.D. 1284; however, there are few tree-ring dates for upper deposits at the pueblo (Watson and others 1980: 207). Based on surface and excavated ceramics, the pueblo was occupied from about A.D. 1275 to 1375 (Table 1.1; Huntley and Kintigh 2004, Appendix), although CARP researchers argue that it was

abandoned earlier (Watson and others 1980: 207). Kintigh (1985a: 51) cites evidence for an earlier structure beneath the main pueblo and suggests that the major occupation associated with the planned construction of the pueblo started around A.D. 1300.

Atsinna Pueblo

The pueblo of Atsinna (LA99; CS 149) is located atop Inscription Rock in the El Morro Valley (Fig. 1.1). Like Pueblo de los Muertos, the shape of Atsinna is rectangular (Fig. 1.3). A double row of rooms encloses three sides and a great kiva is located in the northeast portion of the pueblo. Atsinna and Pueblo de los Muertos also appear to share construction methods (Watson and others 1980). Two or three walls were initially constructed and then subdivided into groups of

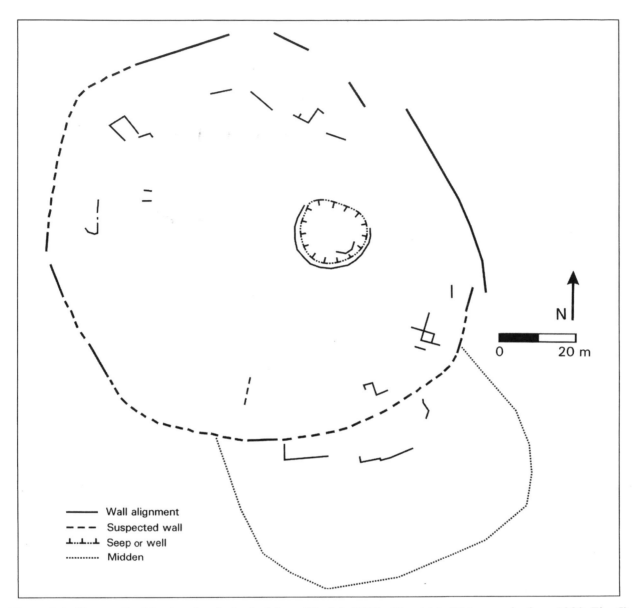

Figure 1.4. Cienega Pueblo site plan (redrafted from Kintigh 1985a, Fig. 4.30; Watson and others 1980, Fig. 5).

rooms that extended from the back wall of the pueblo to the central plaza (LeBlanc 2001: 33). Kintigh (1985a: 52) estimates that the final configuration of this pueblo contained 875 rooms.

In 1952 and 1953, Richard and Nathalie Woodbury (1956) excavated a number of rooms and a kiva at Atsinna. CARP investigators later excavated trenches in two external middens and in the trash-filled plaza (Watson and others 1980). These two investigations produced tree-ring cutting dates of A.D. 1274, 1285 and 1288, as well as non-cutting dates as late as A.D. 1349 (Kintigh 1985a: 52; Watson and others 1980: 207). The

available tree-ring dates and ceramic typological data suggest that Atsinna was constructed and occupied between A.D. 1275 and 1385 (Table 1.1; Huntley and Kintigh 2004, Appendix).

Cienega Pueblo

Cienega Pueblo (LA425; CS 140) is located in the center of the El Morro Valley (Fig. 1.1). The pueblo is oval (Fig. 1.4), probably contained about 500 rooms (Kintigh 1985a: 48), and appears to have been constructed in the A.D. 1280s and later expanded (Watson

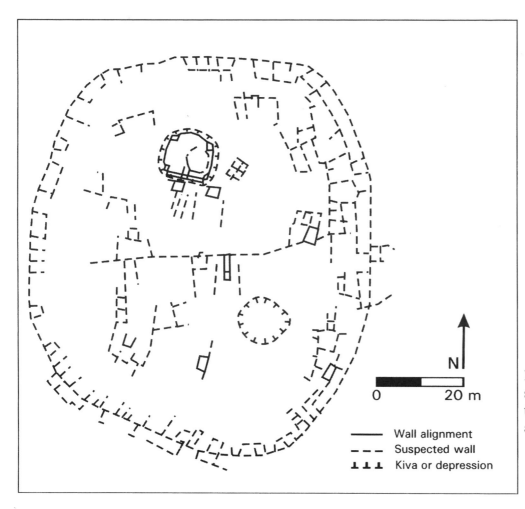

Figure 1.5. Mirabal Pueblo site plan (redrafted from Kintigh 1985a, Fig. 4.24; Watson and others 1980, Fig. 6).

——— Wall alignment
- - - Suspected wall
⊥⊥⊥ Kiva or depression

and others 1980). This expansion involved adding rooms within the plaza that partially covered abandoned, trash-filled rooms. A seep or well in the central part of the plaza, which gives the pueblo its name, is still evident.

CARP excavated 12 units at Cienega, placed mainly in trash-filled rooms within the room block and plaza. The excavations produced three tree-ring cutting dates of A.D. 1279, 1282, and 1287 (Watson and others 1980: 207). Ceramics indicate an occupation span of A.D. 1275 to 1375 (Table 1.1; Huntley and Kintigh 2004, Appendix).

Mirabal Pueblo

The pueblo of Mirabal (LA426; CS 141) is located about 300 m southwest of Cienega in the El Morro Valley (Fig. 1.1). It, too, is oval in shape, but has a unique east-west wall that bisects the pueblo (Fig. 1.5).

A D-shaped kiva is in the northern half of the plaza. Kintigh (1985a: 42) estimates that this pueblo contained as many as 743 two-story rooms. CARP placed excavation units in several rooms, the kiva, and plaza trash. One cutting date of A.D. 1260 and a cluster of four cutting dates between A.D. 1279 and 1286 resulted from the excavation (Watson and others 1980: 207). The main occupation appears to have been from some time around A.D. 1275 to about 1325 (Table 1.1; Huntley and Kintigh 2004, Appendix), although the sampled ceramic assemblage may date to the early end of this time period (Chapter 2).

Heshotauthla Pueblo

Heshotauthla Pueblo (LA15606) is about 20 km (12.4 miles) east of modern Zuni (Fig. 1.1), is roughly oval in overall plan (Fig. 1.6), and contained approximately 875 rooms (Kintigh 1985a: 56). Frederick Webb

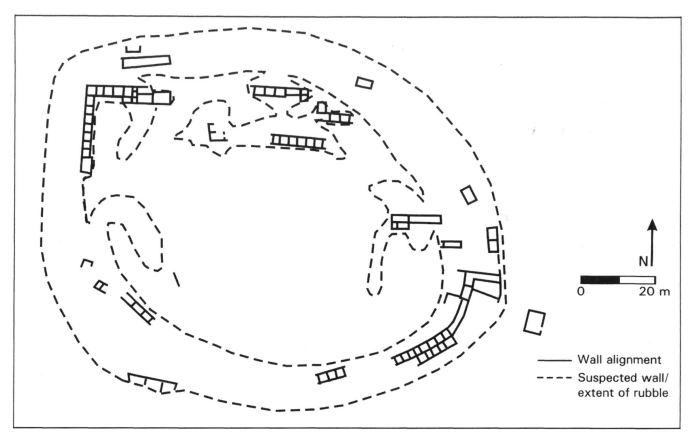

Figure 1.6. Heshotauthla Pueblo site plan (redrafted from Kintigh 1985a, Fig. 4.28 after Fewkes 1891).

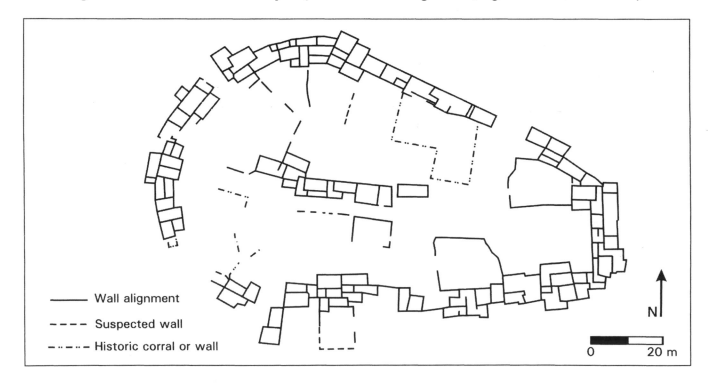

Figure 1.7. Lower Pescado Village site plan (redrafted from Kintigh 1985a, Fig. 4.35; Mindeleff 1891, Fig. 18).

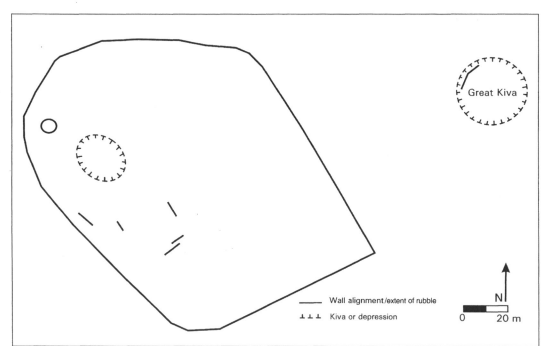

Figure 1.8. Box S Pueblo site plan (redrafted from Kintigh 1997).

Great Kiva

——— Wall alignment/extent of rubble
⊥ ⊥ ⊥ Kiva or depression

N
0   20 m

Hodge, under the direction of Frank Cushing, conducted the first excavations at Heshotauthla in 1888–1889 as part of the Hemenway Expedition. Keith Kintigh later directed the Heshotauthla Archaeological Research Project (HARP) as part of an Arizona State University (ASU) field school in 1990 and 1991. The ASU team excavated 16 test units in trash-filled rooms, a kiva, trash midden, and extramural contexts. There are no tree-ring cutting dates for Heshotauthla, but non-cutting dates cluster between A.D. 1247 and 1291. Available ceramic evidence suggests that Heshotauthla was occupied from about A.D. 1275 to 1385 (Table 1.1; Huntley and Kintigh 2004, Appendix), although the ASU excavations uncovered evidence of an earlier occupation beneath portions of the pueblo (see also Kintigh and others 2004; Zier 1976).

Lower Pescado Village

Lower Pescado Village (ZAP:NM:12:I3:109) is located along the Pescado River just east of Heshotauthla Pueblo and 25 km (15.5 miles) east of modern Zuni Pueblo (Fig. 1.1). Nan Rothschild and Susan Dublin directed excavations at this pueblo in 1990 as part of the Columbia University/Barnard College Archaeological Field School (Rothschild and Dublin 1995). These excavations focused on areas of the pueblo that were threatened by erosion. Ten units were placed in rooms,

trash middens, and other prehistoric and historic features (Rothschild and Dublin 1995, Table 11).

Lower Pescado Village differs from the other pueblos included in this study in that the prehistoric component is overlain by a substantial historic occupation. For this reason, its prehistoric configuration is difficult to determine, although it appears to have been roughly oval in shape (Fig. 1.7). The number of prehistoric rooms is estimated at around 420 (Kintigh 1985a: 53), and the Columbia excavations indicate that the prehistoric component of the pueblo may date as early as the twelfth century and certainly to the fourteenth century (Rothschild and Dublin 1995: 19). Dating of the prehistoric component is based entirely on ceramics; no tree-ring dates are available (Table 1.1; Huntley and Kintigh 2004, Appendix).

Box S Pueblo

Box S Pueblo (LA5538), in the northern portion of the Zuni reservation (Fig. 1.1), is roughly rectangular (Fig. 1.8) and apparently contained more than 1,000 two-story rooms (Kintigh 1997). Keith Kintigh directed a mapping project in 1997 to document the extent of looting present at this pueblo, during which the field crew made the following observations. The site's perimeter was apparently formed by a row of rooms that were two stories high in most places. On the eastern side

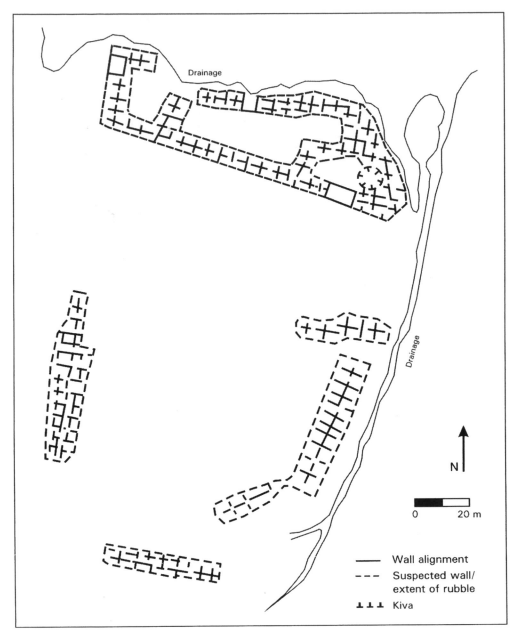

Figure 1.9. Ojo Bonito Pueblo site plan (redrafted from Spier 1918, Fig. 6a). Scale and orientation are approximate.

of the pueblo there was a double wall, as well as an architectural addition outside the exterior wall. An unroofed, oversized great kiva some 28 m in diameter was located across the arroyo and about 70 m east of the main room block. Based on surface ceramics (no tree-ring dates are available), the pueblo's large size, and the presence of the oversized great kiva, Box S probably dates from about A.D. 1225 to 1290 (Table 1.1; Huntley and Kintigh 2004, Appendix).

Ojo Bonito Pueblo

Ojo Bonito (LA11433) consists of a rectangular, plaza-oriented room block and four smaller additional linear room blocks (Fig. 1.9; Fowler and others 1987: 152). The main room block is situated at the edge of a bench above a walled-in spring along Jaralosa Draw in the southwestern portion of the Zuni reservation (Fig. 1.1). Ojo Bonito was probably occupied between A.D.

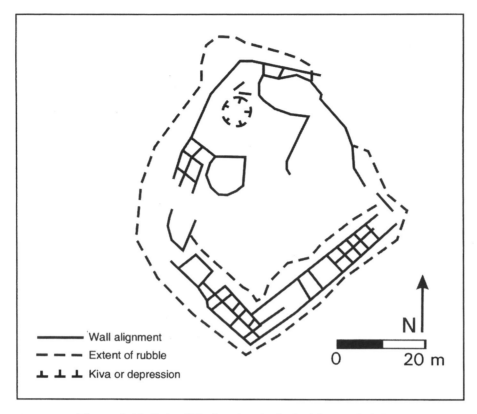

Figure 1.10. Spier 170 site plan (redrafted from Kintigh 2003).

1300 and 1385 and contained around 225 rooms (Table 1.1; Huntley and Kintigh 2004, Appendix). Ceramics from Ojo Bonito came from limited test excavations and surface collections conducted by ASU in 1987 and 1994. I include this pueblo and Spier 170 because Duff (1999, 2002) performed compositional analysis on ceramics from these collections as part of his dissertation research.

Spier 170

Spier 170 (no LA number) is a large sandstone masonry pueblo located along a major side drainage to Jaralosa Draw (Fig. 1.1). The pueblo is well preserved and consisted of a single room block with what appears to have been a central plaza (Fig. 1.10). The overall layout was roughly trapezoidal in shape with a base (southeast side of room block) about 36 m in length, a southwest side approximately 24 m long and a northeast side about 48 m long. The northwest side was bounded by an irregular outer wall about 56 m long. The pueblo was probably occupied between A.D. 1300 and 1385 and contained approximately 200 rooms (Table 1.1; Huntley

and Kintigh 2004, Appendix). ASU researchers led by Keith Kintigh mapped and collected surface samples at Spier 170 in 1988.

PUEBLO IV ORGANIZATIONAL SCALE

Various explanations have been advanced for the organizational parameters of Pueblo IV period regions. They revolve around three major organizational scenarios: autonomy, alliances or polities, and centralization. Although some of these scenarios are commonly used by scholars working outside the Zuni region, they nevertheless provide general heuristic models for interpreting the analyses presented here in subsequent chapters.

Some scholars propose that the architecturally bounded, inwardly focused layout of Pueblo IV period nucleated pueblos reflects a desire to define social group boundaries and promote community integration (Bernardini 1998; Potter 1998). That desire may have been achieved by fostering a strong sense of group identity that emphasized internal solidarity and deemphasized external relations (Bernardini 1998; LeBlanc 1998; S.

Plog and Solometo 1997; Reid and Whittlesey 1999). For example, Bernardini (1998) uses an analysis of the structure of Pueblo IV architectural space to argue that early nucleation (about A.D. 1280–1400 according to Bernardini), particularly in the Western Pueblo area, was characterized by control over both internal and external interactions. Architectural features found at many nucleated pueblos, such as a central plaza surrounded by room blocks, continuous outer walls, and defensive locations, point to a concern with monitoring outside contact. The emphasis on community solidarity may also have been reinforced by the development of the Kachina religion, with its focus on community integration through ritual activities (Adams 1991; Crown 1994).

A related hypothesis is that concentration of Pueblo IV populations into nucleated pueblos and an emphasis on community integration were responses to increasing population density and conflicts over resources (LeBlanc 1989, 1999, 2001; S. Plog and Solometo 1997; Wilcox and Haas 1994). For the Zuni region in particular, some scholars argue that competition over limited resources and the threat of violent intergroup conflicts led to population nucleation as a defensive mechanism (LeBlanc 1978, 1999, 2000, 2001; Watson and others 1980).

Alliance models (as I broadly categorize them here) take various forms; most focus on the potential for regional integration in the absence of centralized political authority. Such regional integration is conceptualized as relatively fluid, informal, and nonhierarchical, with social interactions designed to buffer subsistence risk, mediate conflict, and foster intergroup cooperation (Habicht-Mauche 1993; Levy 1994; Spielmann 1994). Archaeological evidence exists for multipueblo alliances at a number of scales, including entire archaeological regions and pueblo clusters within regions (Adams and Duff 2004; Hegmon 2000).

Habicht-Mauche (1993) argues that a process of tribalization involving informal social and economic ties among large pueblos arose in the Rio Grande Valley as a means to buffer subsistence uncertainty. Similarly, Spielmann (1994) proposes that informal political alliances, or confederacies, involving clusters of Rio Grande pueblos may have developed as a means of mediating conflicts over resources. LeBlanc (2000) emphasizes warfare in making his case for alliances among nucleated pueblos. He argues that a number of independent polities existed within the Zuni region

during the late prehistoric period. These polities supposedly integrated several nucleated pueblos within pueblo clusters into relatively weak and transitory alliances for defensive purposes. Other researchers postulate more hierarchical alliance organization based on interactions among unequal polities (for example, Wilcox 1981, 1991 for the Rio Grande pueblos).

Complementarity represents a particular kind of alliance between pairs (or perhaps small groups) of nucleated pueblos. In this case, pueblo clusters are made up of autonomous "mother" pueblos and dependent colony pueblos with variable local histories. "Mother" and "daughter" pueblos may also differ in size. This type of organization has been described for ethnohistoric pueblos such as Hopi (Whiteley 1988) and also appears to have existed among Pueblo IV nucleated pueblos in the Jumanos cluster east of the Rio Grande Valley (W. Graves 1996, 2002). A more symmetrical form of ritual complementarity is appropriate for Pueblo IV Zuni region pueblos, which do not appear to have varied dramatically in size.

Potter (1997), focusing on changes in status differentiation during the Pueblo III to Pueblo IV transition (A.D. 1250–1300), suggests that pairs of nucleated pueblos in the eastern part of the Zuni region were characterized by close social and political relationships resulting from ritual interdependency. Evidence for interdependency includes differential distributions of ritually significant avifauna, that is, waterfowl at oval pueblos versus raptors at rectangular pueblos (Potter 1997; Potter and Perry 2000). The pairing of oval and rectangular pueblos is interpreted as a symbolic representation of dualistic (although not necessarily equal) ritual relationships (Potter and Perry 2000: 75).

Upham (1982) and others (Upham and Reed 1989) have advanced a centralized model for Pueblo IV sociopolitical organization. According to their interpretation, regional sociopolitical entities, or alliances, consisted of several nucleated pueblos that were integrated by a centralized political and economic organization managed by elites. Decorated pots produced at the center of each alliance served as status markers for elites, who managed the exchange of these items.

The validity of a centralized model, as it was originally conceived by Upham (1982), has been repeatedly questioned, largely due to misinterpretations of the available archaeological evidence. In particular, the apparent differential distribution of decorated pottery among pueblos within particular regions was based on the assumed contemporaneity of many pueblos that now are believed to date to different time periods (Duff 1999, 2002). Nevertheless, the centralized model is still present in the Southwestern literature, and various scholars continue to critique it (Duff 1999, 2002; McGuire and Saitta 1996; Neitzel 1999). For this reason I include it here in hopes of addressing its applicability (or lack thereof) to the Zuni region.

One characteristic that various organizational scenarios have in common is that they tend to focus on the political and economic components of intergroup relationships. Thus, to predict or assess those kinds of interactions in prehistory requires archaeologically detectable material correlates such as evidence for interpueblo exchange transactions or similarities in the physical properties of material culture, like pottery.

CHAPTER TWO

Production and Distribution of Ancestral Zuni Glaze-Decorated Pottery

Ceramics, as well as other forms of material culture, are imbued with conscious and unconscious information pertaining to social relationships resulting from their manufacture, use, and exchange (Costin 1998; Lemonnier 1992, 1993; Sackett 1977; Wiessner 1985; Wobst 1977). Pottery production arrangements in the Zuni region reveal interactions among producers that can be used to define potters' "communities of practice." Identifiable practices include resource use, development of glaze recipes, and certain aspects of stylistic behavior. By taking into account pottery use contexts and mechanisms by which vessels are circulated, pottery exchange systems can be used as a proxy for social interactions among consumers (Abbott 1996; Allen 1984; M. Graves 1994; Sahlins 1972). The nature and intensity of various interactions between and among producers and consumers, in turn, helps to define scales of regional integration.

I begin by describing the analyzed ceramic types, then evaluate the current understanding of ancestral Zuni glaze-decorated vessel production, use, and distribution. Next I discuss sampling methods and conclude with an overview of my previous seriation of decorated ceramic assemblages from the archaeological sites included in this study. The seriation indicates that early and late archaeological contexts can be identified within the larger sample. These temporal distinctions are used throughout this book in subsequent analyses of ceramic production and exchange.

PRODUCTION, EXCHANGE, AND INTERACTION

What does it mean when groups of people construct and decorate their pottery in the same way? The answer varies depending on the organization of production (for example, whether it is at the level of the individual household or controlled by craft specialists) and on the demand for and use contexts of particular vessel types. Ceramic production arrangements denote one set of social relationships; ceramic distribution systems denote another. Thus, in middle-range societies of the American Southwest, production, context of use, and distribution mechanisms are interconnected. Understanding these parameters and their interrelationships is one way to evaluate organizational variability in regional social and economic institutions, as well as producers' and consumers' social affiliations.

Production Organization

Ethnographic and archaeological studies of prehistoric Southwestern societies suggest that pottery production is typically organized at the household level (Hagstrum 1995; Mills and Crown 1995), although groups of households or other kin may cooperate in some production activities, especially firing (Bernardini 2000; Blinman and Swink 1997). With household or domestic mode production (Sahlins 1972), vessels are made as needed for use within the immediate household (Rice 1987: 184). A variation on domestic production is the household industry, wherein individuals invest additional labor (but still work only part-time) to produce a surplus of pottery for consumption outside the immediate household (Mills 2000: 332; Rice 1987: 184; see also Costin 1991: 8–9 regarding individual specialization).

For the American Southwest, there is abundant evidence that particular households or pueblos engaged in low-level household industry specialization during particular time periods (Mills and Crown 1995). Decades of petrographic studies by Shepard (1942), Warren (1969, 1981), and others (Capone 1997, 2006; Herhahn 1995; Nelson and Habicht-Mauche 2006) have demonstrated shifts in Rio Grande glaze-decorated vessel production centers through time, with villages such as San Marcos Pueblo in the Galisteo Basin producing large numbers of widely distributed glaze-decorated vessels. Household industry production for exchange is also known from the Classic period Hohokam region (Abbott 1996, 2000; Abbott and Walsh-Anduze 1995). In the absence of direct evidence for pottery production at most Southwestern sites (such as kilns and production debris), identifying prehistoric pottery production systems is largely dependent on chemical characterization techniques (Abbott 1996, 2000; Adams and others 1993; Bishop and others 1982; Bishop and others 1988; Burton and Simon 1993; Crown 1994; Duff 1999, 2002; Glowacki and Neff 2002; Mills and Crown 1995; Simon and others 1998; Triadan 1997; Zedeño 1994).

Because pottery production is embedded within larger cultural systems, we can conceptualize interactions within and among groups of affiliated potters in terms of learning frameworks, or communities of practice. Following Lave and Wenger (1991: 50), Minar (2001), and Wenger (1998: 45), members of communities of practice are considered to be similar ethnically or participants in other close-knit social groups within which particular manufacturing techniques are learned and perpetuated. In Pueblo society, interactions among women largely structure potters' communities of practice, because women traditionally produce most of the pottery (Bunzel 1972; Crown and Wills 1995; Hays-Gilpin 2000; Mills 1995, 2000).

One way to identify communities of practice archaeologically is to examine those aspects of pottery manufacture that may be unconscious and that likely reflect face-to-face learning contexts and enculturation processes. Shared manufacturing techniques might be considered "social representations," defined by Lemonnier (1992: 79) as "sets of ideas shared by members of a given social group," and consist of both implicit and explicit contexts. Implicit contexts include unconscious mental operations, such as the movement of hands and fingers when forming a pot, whereas explicit contexts incorporate specific technical knowledge and the symbolic or communicative aspect of technology (Lemonnier 1992: 80–81). Implicit contexts, similar to Carr's (1995) low visibility stylistic attributes, also include selection and preparation of clays and other resources not wholly constrained by functional requirements.

Identifying symbolic or communicative behavior expressed in material culture, subsumed under the rubric of style, is another way of identifying communities of

practice. Although opinions vary greatly as to how to define style, many researchers agree that stylistic behavior, such as pottery decoration, can convey meaningful social information, including conceptions of group affiliation (Dietler and Herbich 1989, 1998; Gosselain 1998, 2000; M. Graves 1994; Hegmon 1998; Sackett 1990; Wiessner 1983, 1984, 1985, 1990; Wobst 1977). Carr's (1995: 195-198) high visibility ceramic attributes, including surface treatment and painted decoration, are examples of stylistic elements likely to convey information about social identity or group membership. A critical aspect of decorative style is that it operates simultaneously in multiple dimensions and thus is context specific (DeBoer 1990: 83; Wobst 1977). Anthropologists and archaeologists who study style must carefully consider for whom stylistic messages are intended within a given context. For example, David and his colleagues (1988) argue that the decoration of North African Mafa and Bulahay pottery serves, in part, to remind individuals who come into contact with it on a daily basis of essential religious and cosmological principles.

Ancestral Zuni Kwakina Polychrome, along with matte-painted Pinto Polychrome in the Salado tradition, appears to be the earliest example of a distinctive new style of polychrome pottery that appeared suddenly across most of the northern Southwest (Crown 1994: 17–18; Kintigh 1985a: 15). In her notable study of Salado Polychrome, Crown (1994) argues that this particular use of slip color combinations and the Pinedale design style (used on some ancestral Zuni glaze-decorated vessels and related to the Heshotauthla design style) was associated with the adoption of a Southwestern Regional Cult. She proposes that, on the one hand, widespread adoption of the style reflects large-scale integration of diverse social groups through participation in the cult. On the other hand, different color combinations on vessels decorated in the Pinedale style suggest that expressions of social group differences continued to be important to some and that the level of participation in the cult varied from group to group. Similarly, W. Graves and Eckert (1998: 276) and Mobley-Tanaka (1998: 10) report that pottery specialists from various Rio Grande Valley production centers used a limited repertoire of designs to paint their glaze-decorated vessels. These researchers interpret this phenomenon as evidence for a shared iconic system associated with the adoption of a new, widespread religious ideology in the A.D. 1300s. Participation in this system would have been reinforced each time Rio Grande glaze-decorated vessels were used or viewed.

Complicating the archaeological study of communities of practice is the recognition that various cross-cutting affiliations influence technological and stylistic choices made by groups of interacting potters (Sassaman and Rudolphi 2001). Moreover, potters commonly participate in multiple communities of practice (MacEachern 1998; Sassaman and Rudolphi 2001). MacEachern (1998) shows that female potters in the Mandara region of Nigeria and Cameroon frequently remarry and live in many different villages during their lifetimes, often crossing ethnic boundaries to do so. Variability in pottery traditions within the region does not, therefore, correspond to the distribution of ethnic groups across the landscape, but rather more accurately reflects the ever-changing associations of potters with different learning communities (although MacEachern does not put it in exactly these terms). A similar phenomenon is reported among Hopi potters, who may change pottery manufacturing techniques and use of specific designs during the course of their lifetimes based on their associations with other potters (Stanislawski 1978). Chilton (1998) shows that there are major differences between Algonquian and Iroquois pottery technology and decorative styles, despite probable interaction and information sharing between the two groups. She argues that this pattern is a result of the conscious effort on the part of both groups to maintain social distinctions. Stark and others (1998) examine patterns of domestic architecture, settlement morphology, and attributes of utilitarian ceramics from the Tonto Basin of central Arizona in order to track variability in the expression of social boundaries during the Hohokam Classic period. They argue this variability points to the co-residence of distinct cultural or ethnic populations within particular communities, or bounded "local systems," within which regular face-to-face interactions were concentrated (Stark and others 1998: 208). These studies demonstrate that, despite potential difficulties in identifying material signatures of interaction, we can develop expectations as to what kinds of evidence regularly interacting communities of practice might leave in the archaeological record.

Demand

The status of prehistoric Southwestern ceramic containers as socially valuable items, rather than only as materially valuable commodities, is an important factor to keep in mind when evaluating the demand for extra-household products. In general, pottery vessels are normally considered low-value, utilitarian goods rather than items of wealth (Arnold 1985; Spielmann 2000: 374). This low tangible value, however, does not preclude pottery from conveying meaningful social or symbolic information or exclude pots from use in social negotiations (Cumberpatch and Blinkhorn 1997; Mills 2000; Stark 1998a, Stark 1998b).

Although Upham (1982) has argued that late prehistoric Western Pueblo decorated vessels were "elite" wares made by craft specialists, the fact that they are universally found in association with domestic refuse at excavated Pueblo IV sites suggests that they were commonly used in everyday domestic contexts. Domestic use, however, does not preclude use in ceremonial contexts or other social situations, as well. As Mills (1999b: 104, 2000: 308) points out in her discussion of the social contexts of cuisine in the American Southwest, Pueblo ceremonies traditionally involved the preparation, transport, and serving of feast foods using ceramic containers. Further, Mills (2007) states that red-slipped bowls with bold exterior designs were used to actively signal shared social identity. Pueblo IV period glaze-decorated bowls presumably played an important role in the development of new ritual activities, such as communal feasts, in the Rio Grande Valley (Spielmann 1998; W. Graves and Spielmann 2000). Evidence for communal feasting includes the association of glaze-decorated bowls with artifacts and ecofacts related to ritual food preparation and consumption, such as non-subsistence fauna, at Quarai Pueblo in the Salinas district (Spielmann 1998: 256). Pueblo ethnography and some archaeological evidence indicate that particular Pueblo decorated vessel forms were also used in more esoteric contexts, such as containers of sacred objects in ritual activities (Dutton 1963; Goldfrank 1970; Hibben 1975; Smith 1952; Stevenson 1904). Such use may also have fueled the demand for certain types of ceramic containers.

Exchange

In a review of the motivations and mechanisms for ceramic circulation in the American Southwest, Zedeño (1998) critiques the longstanding view that exchange is largely intended to buffer risk and manage scarce resources. She offers several alternative scenarios for the movement of ceramic vessels across the landscape, including residential mobility and exchange as ways of maintaining social relationships. One key point that emerges from Zedeño's discussion is that all movement of pottery, at least in the prehistoric Southwest, must also have involved the movement of people, be it across the landscape or across the plaza. Another important point is that exchange transactions in middle-range societies occur in a variety of contexts of interaction, ranging from face-to-face informal contact between friends or relatives (Braun and Plog 1982; S. Plog 1980; Sahlins 1972), to more formalized exchanges, such as those associated with ceremonial offerings, gifts, bridewealth, feasts, public ceremonies, markets, or trade fairs (Zedeño 1998), to cementing alliances in a ritual context (Abbott 1996; Blinman 1989). Ceramic exchange may occur across relatively long distances, as in the movement of Hopi Yellow Ware to settlements along the Upper Little Colorado River drainage (Duff 1999, 2002) or across fairly short distances, as in the exchange of locally produced Salado Polychrome vessels among Tonto Basin settlements (Simon and others 1998).

Archaeological and ethnographic evidence indicates that plain and decorated vessels are often exchanged in different contexts and signal different kinds of social transactions (Abbott 2000; Blinman 1989; Brunson 1985; Duff 1999, 2002; Zedeño 1998). Plain or utility ware tends to be exchanged among closely affiliated individuals or social groups in informal contexts that include gift giving and bartering (Duff 2002: 27; M. Graves 1991; Stark 1992). Reciprocal exchanges such as these fulfill social, political, and ceremonial obligations among closely interacting individuals or groups (Sahlins 1972). Thus, patterns of utility ware exchange may elucidate local networks of social interaction (Abbott 2000; Brunson 1985; Capone 1997; Van Keuren and others 1997). Among the Philippine Kalinga, for example, utilitarian cooking, storage, and serving vessels are widely circulated via gift giving and barter, typically among women sharing real or fictive bonds of kinship (M. Graves 1991; Stark 1992).

Within ancestral Pueblo society, decorated vessels probably were more highly valued than utility ware and likely circulated through relatively broad networks of interaction involving regional or long-distance exchanges in formal social and ritual contexts (Blinman 1989; Duff 2002; Spielmann 1998; Zedeño 1998). In the Rio Grande Valley, for example, researchers have

suggested that community-level specialization was linked to the emergence of a complex, highly interdependent regional economy (Habicht-Mauche 1993, 1995; Snow 1981). Under this economic system, Rio Grande glaze-decorated vessels, once relatively low-value "generalized reciprocal gift items," became a sought-after commodity (Habicht-Mauche 1993: 98, 1995: 192). Their new social status may have been reflected in new contexts of distribution among spatially and socially distant groups, including formalized reciprocity (for example, ceremonial offerings, gifts, bridewealth, feasts, and public ceremonies), as well as barter exchanges such as trade fairs (Clark 2006: 29). Contributing glaze-decorated vessels for use in public ceremonies may have conferred prestige to individual potters, their households, or entire communities (W. Graves 1996, 2002, 2004; W. Graves and Spielmann 2000).

ANCESTRAL ZUNI GLAZE-DECORATED POTTERY

Zuni glaze-decorated pottery is one example of an innovative class of ceramics decorated with vitreous paint that was made across the northern Southwest for a long interval extending into the sixteenth century. Although traditionally referred to as "Zuni Glaze Ware," these vessels do not have all-over glazed surfaces, but rather are decorated with glazed linework. Thus, I use the term "glaze-decorated" throughout this volume to refer to Zuni series types and similar varieties with glaze paint designs. Below I summarize the typological attributes for Heshotauthla Polychrome and Kwakina Polychrome, and their antecedent White Mountain Red Ware type, St. Johns Polychrome, all made during the early Pueblo IV period, and review the results of previous studies of ceramic production and exchange in the Zuni region (Duff 1999, 2002; Mills 1995; Stone 1992, 1994, 1999).

Type Descriptions

St. Johns Polychrome (Figs. 2.1–2.3) of the White Mountain Red Ware series (Carlson 1970; Seventh Southwestern Ceramic Seminar 1965) was apparently produced throughout much of central Arizona and New Mexico and was common in the Zuni region between A.D. 1200 and 1300 (Kintigh 1985a). Potters began experimenting with glaze paints toward the end of this

Figure 2.1. St. Johns Polychrome bowl (black-on-red-interior).

Figure 2.3. St. Johns Polychrome bowl (black-on-red interior).

Figure 2.2. Exterior of St. Johns Polychrome bowl in Figure 2.1, showing white-on-red exterior.

Figure 2.4. Heshotauthla Polychrome bowl (black-on-red interior; rim diameter is 35.3 cm).

time period, and St. Johns Polychrome vessels exhibit a wide range of paint textures, from matte mineral paints to well-vitrified glazes. Some St. Johns Polychrome vessels are difficult to distinguish from Heshotauthla Polychrome, and analysts frequently use the width of exterior white lines (wide for St. Johns Polychrome, narrow for Heshotauthla Polychrome) to classify them. St. Johns Polychrome bowls are typically slipped red or orange on both the exterior and interior, with black interior designs in the Tularosa style and exterior white geometric designs (Carlson 1970). St.

Johns Black-on-red is a variant that lacks exterior white paint.

Heshotauthla Polychrome (Figs. 2.4, 2.5) and Kwakina Polychrome (Figs. 2.6–2.8) were made in the late thirteenth through fourteenth centuries and are most

Figure 2.5. Heshotauthla Polychrome bowl (black-on-red interior; rule is 15 cm long).

Figure 2.7. Kwakina Polychrome bowl (black and white-on-red interior).

Figure 2.6. Kwakina Polychrome bowl (black-on-white interior).

Figure 2.8. Kwakina Polychrome bowl, showing exterior of Figure 2.7 vessel.

commonly bowl forms (Carlson 1970; Eckert 2006; Kintigh 1985a; Woodbury and Woodbury 1966; Zier 1976). Both types are traditionally considered to belong to the White Mountain Red Ware series (Carlson 1970); however, they are distinguished by stylistic attributes (such as design layout and color scheme) that can be considered unique to the Zuni and Upper Little

Colorado River regions (Eckert 2006). For this reason, I follow Duff (1999, 2002), Eckert (2006), Mills (1999a) and Woodbury and Woodbury (1966) in referring to these two types as early or ancestral Zuni (to distinguish them from historic Zuni glaze vessels).

Heshotauthla Polychrome (Figs. 2.4, 2.5) is typically slipped bright red or orange on both the interior and exterior with a Heshotauthla style interior glaze-painted design (Carlson 1970; Eckert 2006; Seventh Southwestern Ceramic Seminar 1965). The polychrome version has thin, white geometric line designs on the exterior; the Heshotauthla Black-on-red variant lacks exterior white lines. Heshotauthla Polychrome was made between about A.D. 1275 and 1400 (Eckert 2006; Kintigh 1985a; Woodbury and Woodbury 1966). According to Eckert (2006: 40–41), Heshotauthla style has designs normally laid out in a thin band, often divided into quarters, around a circular open base; designs are usually geometric with more painted surface than unpainted (creating a "negative" effect), often incorporating solid fill, "eyes," lightning, and stepped motifs. Unlike the Pinedale style (Carlson 1970; Crown 1994), hatched motifs are rarely used in the Heshotauthla style.

Kwakina Polychrome (Figs. 2.6–2.8) bowls are white-slipped on the interior and red- or orange-slipped on the exterior (Carlson 1970; Eckert 2006; Woodbury and Woodbury 1966). Interior glaze paint designs typically appear in Tularosa, Pinedale, or Heshotauthla design styles (Carlson 1970). Exterior designs are often formed by thin, white geometric lines nearly identical to those on Heshotauthla Polychrome. Production dates are probably the same as for Heshotauthla Polychrome, although Kintigh (1985a, Table 3.1) proposes that initial production dates for Kwakina Polychrome are slightly earlier than for Heshotauthla Polychrome.

Keith Kintigh and I suggest (Huntley and Kintigh 2004: 70) that the circulation of Kwakina Polychrome within the Zuni region is socially meaningful in that it is differentially distributed among pueblos with oval versus rectangular architectural layouts. We compared the proportion of Kwakina Polychrome to the proportion of all glaze-on-red and polychrome types (St. Johns, Springerville, Heshotauthla, and Kwakina) in early versus late Pueblo IV components as defined by ceramic seriation (see below).

In early contexts, two rectangular sites in the El Morro Valley (Atsinna and Pueblo de los Muertos) contain substantially higher proportions of Kwakina Polychrome than two El Morro Valley oval sites (Cienega and Mirabal) and oval Heshotauthla Pueblo, located in the Pescado Basin. The late component pattern is completely different and shows even more variation in the distribution of Kwakina Polychrome. Based on this pattern, we propose (Huntley and Kintigh 2004: 70) that variability in the distribution of Kwakina Polychrome indicates intraregional differentiation in social group

membership or religious practices that were manifested during the initial formation of the nucleated pueblos.

Previous Compositional Studies

Little is known about the production and exchange of ancestral Zuni glaze-decorated vessels. Initially, researchers speculated that the manufacture of Heshotauthla Polychrome and Kwakina Polychrome was limited to a few settlements in the "core" of the Zuni region near present-day Zuni Pueblo or in the El Morro Valley (Carlson 1970; Woodbury and Woodbury 1966). However, Duff (1999, 2002) has shown that ancestral Zuni glaze-decorated vessels were also produced in the Upper Little Colorado River drainage and are commonly found in that area. Although ancestral Zuni types occur in low frequencies at some Mogollon Rim sites, such as Bailey Ruin, they were presumably not made there (Mills 1999a: 259). Similar types with minor differences in slip colors and design motifs are also found in the Ácoma region (Dittert 1959; Eckert 2006; Schachner 2006; Seventh Southwestern Ceramic Seminar 1965), where production and distribution systems also are poorly understood.

Chemical compositional analyses of ceramics and clays from the Zuni region and adjacent areas have successfully identified distinctive compositional groups that can be linked to particular production areas occupying different geological provinces. These analyses also indicate changes through time in the intensity of ceramic exchange and interaction. Studies by Stone (1992, 1994, 1999), Duff (1999, 2002), and Mills (1995) are most relevant to this research.

Stone (1992, 1994, 1999) uses a weak acid extraction method with inductively coupled plasma emission spectrography (see Burton and Simon 1993 for a review of this method) to determine the chemical compositions of White Mountain Red Ware and Cibola White Ware dating to the twelfth through fourteenth centuries. Her analysis includes ceramics from several sites in the El Morro Valley, the unnamed canyon south of the Pescado drainage, and the Ojo Bonito area (Jaralosa Draw). Stone argues that ceramic exchange among populations residing within these three portions of the Zuni region was extremely rare both prior to and during the regional population aggregation of the A.D. mid–1100s to mid–1200s. Ceramic exchange among later nucleated pueblos (represented in her sample by Heshotauthla and Cienega) was apparently even less common (Stone 1992, Table 6.8). She attributes a notable decline in interregional interaction beginning in the twelfth century (compared with the earlier Chaco period, A.D. 1050–1150) to increasing community isolation, an absence of economic cooperation, and a decrease in communication among nucleated pueblos.

Duff's (1999, 2002) INAA study using decorated ware, utility ware, and raw clays from three pueblos in the El Morro Valley (Atsinna, Cienega, and Pueblo de los Muertos), Heshotauthla Pueblo, and two pueblos located along Jaralosa Draw (Ojo Bonito and Spier 170) largely confirms Stone's conclusions. His study indicates that the movement of both decorated and utility ware vessels within the Zuni region was uncommon during the Pueblo IV period, particularly between El Morro Valley pueblos and other pueblo clusters. Duff identifies four compositional groups, two of which he attributes to the Western province (Jaralosa Draw area), one to the Pescado Basin, and one to the El Morro Valley. Of his sample of 146 sherds, only 12 were recovered from archaeological contexts outside of their presumed production area (Duff 2002: 134). Furthermore, none of those 12 vessels were moved from the eastern portion of the Zuni region to pueblos in the western portion of the region. The limited ceramic exchange that did occur among nucleated pueblos thus appears to have been asymmetrical. Duff attributes the apparently low level of ceramic exchange during the Pueblo IV period to a lack of social interaction among relatively self-sufficient, spatially segregated groups of nucleated pueblos, and he concludes that social interactions were concentrated within the Zuni region during this time.

Mills' (1995) study of sixteenth-century Zuni glaze-decorated vessels from seven protohistoric pueblos in the Zuni River Basin demonstrated a shift in patterns of ceramic production and exchange. During the protohistoric period, ceramic vessels were made from a limited number of compositionally distinct clay sources associated with the Dakota Sandstone Formation. Mills used flame atomic absorption spectroscopy and graphite furnace atomic absorption spectroscopy to chemically characterize 45 Zuni glaze sherds and 48 raw clay samples from the Chinle and Dakota Sandstone formations. The analyses indicated that all but one of the sherds was made from Dakota Sandstone clay (Mills 1995: 213). Mills' comparison of fired clay colors from the two geological formations with Zuni glaze and Matsaki Buff sherd colors also suggested that glaze-

decorated vessels were made from a narrower range of raw materials than buff vessels. Based on these results, she argued that production of protohistoric Zuni glaze-decorated vessels was more specialized than other wares and was perhaps limited to a cluster of five pueblos (Binna:wa, Halona:wa, Ah:kya:ya, Mats'a:kya, and Kyaki:ma) located nearest the Dakota Sandstone clay sources in the eastern portion of the Zuni River Basin. Mills proposed that, at least by the sixteenth century, regularized exchange relationships were in place among Zuni region pueblos and that community-level specialization in the production of particular ceramic types was present at that time.

THE CERAMIC SAMPLE

I sampled decorated and utility ware sherds from nine approximately contemporaneous Zuni region nucleated pueblos (Atsinna, Cienega, Mirabal, Pueblo de los Muertos, Heshotauthla, Lower Pescado Village, Box S Pueblo, Ojo Bonito, and Spier 170). Subsets of the larger samples from each pueblo were used for INAA and for electron microprobe and lead isotope analyses.

General Sampling Considerations

The majority of sampled ceramics came from stratified trash-filled rooms, trash middens, and plaza and kiva deposits. I generally avoided surface sherds unless I needed to increase the sample size for a particular ceramic type. In the case of Box S Pueblo, Ojo Bonito, and Spier 170, little or no excavated material was available and I had to rely on systematically collected surface sherds. My sample, including data generated by other projects, consisted of 465 decorated and utility ware sherds distributed across nine sites, as well as 49 clay samples. From this total I collected INAA, electron microprobe, glaze and slip color, and lead isotope data for subsets of varying sizes. Table 2.1 lists the number of samples from each site that I analyzed using each particular technique, with a breakdown by ceramic type. Individual type and total columns for each analysis exclude a few samples that were analyzed but did not provide usable data. Also, Spier 170 and Ojo Bonito were not originally part of my research design, but I decided to use published INAA data for these sites (Duff 1999, 2002) in my analysis of regional ceramic production and exchange. I did not record any stylistic information or conduct additional compositional analyses on Duff's INAA samples.

Table 2.1. Frequencies of Analyzed Ceramic Types by Site

Site (Total no. of samples)	Heshotauthla Polychrome	Paste Composition (INAA)					Glaze Composition (Electron Microprobe)			
		Kwakina Polychrome	St. Johns Poly.	Utility Ware	Other[1]	Total	Heshotauthla Polychrome	Kwakina Poly.	St. Johns Poly.	Total
Atsinna (63)	18	-	4	11	1	34	33	15	6	54
Cienega (46)	5	6	5	6	1	23	20	10	8	38
Mirabal (45)	4	5	6	7	1	23	12	5	17	34
Pueblo de los Muertos (77)	12	7	4	12	1	36	28	27	10	65
Heshotauthla (64)	13	7	4	12	3	39	26	15	14	55
Lower Pescado Village (63)	10	10	5	10	-	35	29	17	5	51
Box S Pueblo (38)	5	2	11	12	-	30	5	1	10	16
Ojo Bonito[2] (34)	9	10	-	10	11	40	-	-	-	-
Spier 170[2] (35)	12	10	-	10	8	40	-	-	-	-
Clay[3] (49)	-	-	-	-	32	32	-	-	-	-
Total (514)	*88*	*57*	*39*	*90*	*58*	*332*	*153*	*90*	*70*	*313*

	Glaze and Slip Color				Lead Isotopes (Hr ICP-MS)			
	Heshotauthla Polychrome	Kwakina Polychrome	St. Johns Poly.	Total	Heshotauthla Polychrome	Kwakina Poly.	St. Johns Poly.	Total
Atsinna	34	16	7	57	33	16	2	51
Cienega	21	11	8	40	21	8	6	35
Mirabal	13	8	17	38	8	1	7	16
Pueblo de los Muertos	29	29	12	70	27	25	5	57
Heshotauthla	26	16	15	57	26	15	10	51
Lower Pescado Village	29	18	6	53	23	10	1	34
Box S Pueblo	5	2	11	18	1	-	4	5
Total	*157*	*100*	*76*	*333*	*139*	*75*	*35*	*249*

[1] Includes unpublished INAA data from 30 clay samples analyzed by Barbara Mills, 19 additional raw and archaeological clay samples from various areas, and 9 protohistoric Zuni Glaze Ware sherds analyzed by Duff (1999, 2002).
[2] Data from Duff (1999, 2002).
[3] Clay samples not from a particular site.

My main sampling objectives were to maximize the representation of different types from early and late Pueblo IV contexts by site, to select sherds from as many intrasite spatial contexts as possible, and to sample a wide variety of glaze colors. I selected large sherds that had enough glaze paint to conduct multiple kinds of compositional analyses on the same sherd. I began this selection by identifying proveniences within each site that contained sherds of St. Johns, Heshotauthla, and Kwakina polychromes. Next I examined each sherd from the selected proveniences at each site.

Heshotauthla Polychrome was proportionately more common than St. Johns Polychrome or Kwakina Polychrome in the Pueblo IV assemblages from most of the sites that I examined and my sample generally reflected this. My previous ceramic seriation of Heshotauthla Pueblo pottery guided sample selection from excavated proveniences at this site. Large portions of the El Morro Valley site assemblages had also been seriated previously by Marquardt (1974), LeBlanc (1975, 1976, 1978), Duff (1996), Duff and Kintigh (1997), and Potter (1997), and I was able to select sherds from early and late contexts at those sites. Because the Box S surface collection was so small, I analyzed all available sherds with glaze paint from this site. For Lower Pescado Village, I identified general occupation spans for various proveniences based on the excavation report (Rothschild and Dublin 1995).

I also tried to select sherds with paints that exhibited some vitrification (that is, glaze formation). I made an attempt to avoid extremely weathered glazes (because weathering might affect composition), although I did include a number of glazes with variable vitrification that might be considered subglazes. Rather than attempting to systematically sample sherds with particular glaze colors, I selected as wide a variety of colors as possible. In other words, if I encountered an unusual glaze color (for example, purple or red) within the assemblage from a particular provenience, I selected it for analysis. For those sites where purple or red glazes are uncommon or absent in my sample, they were also uncommon or absent in the overall site assemblage. I might have, to some extent, biased my sample toward the more rare or unusual glaze colors but I probably did so for all sites equally. Thus, although the various samples cannot be considered strictly random, they should contain the full range of glaze paint colors and textures within available archaeological contexts from each site.

To control for vessel form and function, I selected bowl rim sherds whenever possible, but bowl body sherds were also used. Duff's INAA sample included a few jar body sherds that I incorporated into my analysis. Sherds from each site were carefully examined (by comparing color, wall thickness, and design) to ensure that multiple sherds from the same vessel were not sampled. With the exception of a few burned or extremely weathered samples, I coded interior glaze color, exterior glaze color (if applicable), glaze texture (matte or shiny) and interior and exterior slip colors for all 333 decorated sherds in my collection (Table 2.1). I did not code this information for sherds from Ojo Bonito and Spier 170 that Duff analyzed (nor did he).

Electron Microprobe Sample

Thick sections for electron microprobe analysis were originally prepared for a total of 333 sherds (157 Heshotauthla Polychrome, 100 Kwakina Polychrome and 76 St. Johns Polychrome). Glaze paint compositional data were obtained for 313 of these samples

(Table 2.1). I included in my microprobe sample 59 decorated sherds previously submitted for INAA of paste composition by Duff (1999, 2002) as part of his dissertation research. Duff's sample consisted primarily of sherds from Pueblo de los Muertos, Atsinna, and Heshotauthla. I also selected additional sherds from Heshotauthla, other El Morro Valley sites, Box S Pueblo, and Lower Pescado Village.

Lead Isotope Sample

I originally planned to select subsets of samples for lead isotope analysis and INAA from glaze compositional groups once I had identified them. However, since the microprobe analysis took much longer than expected, instead I sampled glazes with a range of lead compositions, as determined by the electron microprobe, and at the same time sampled as many archaeological contexts from each site as possible. Of the 333 sherds originally selected for electron microprobe analysis, I prepared 283 sherds for lead isotope analysis using Hr ICP-MS. Of the fifty sherds that I intentionally excluded from the lead isotope analysis, many did not have enough glaze paint remaining after microprobe thick section preparation, despite my efforts to select large sherds. Many also had weathered or matte glazes. A few others were from proveniences (excavation units) represented by multiple sherds. I excluded them to ensure that other proveniences were represented in the lead isotope sample, since funds and time for sample preparation were limited. In addition to the samples that I intentionally excluded, I discovered that low lead levels in a number of acid-digested glaze samples made them unreliable for lead isotope determination (see Chapter 4 for details). Of the 283 samples that I originally prepared for ICP-MS analysis, I obtained lead isotope data for 249 sherds (Table 2.1).

INAA Sample

I submitted a subset of the electron microprobe sample for INAA of paste composition. The main goal of INAA was to build on Duff's (1999, 2002) study, which focused on Heshotauthla and Kwakina polychromes (along with a small number of utility ware and other types) from five sites (Heshotauthla Pueblo, Atsinna, Pueblo de los Muertos, Ojo Bonito, and Spier 170). My study expanded on Duff's original sample of 155 sherds and clays to incorporate an additional 23

Heshotauthla Polychrome, 23 Kwakina Polychrome, 38 St. Johns Polychrome, 55 utility ware sherds, and 8 archaeological and non-archaeological clay samples. I included samples from two El Morro Valley sites (Cienega and Mirabal) not included in Duff's original analysis, as well as samples from Box S Pueblo and Lower Pescado Village. Barbara Mills also provided access to her INAA compositional data for 30 Zuni region clays, bringing the total INAA sample used to track ceramic production and exchange to 332 (Table 2.1).

The high cost of INAA (compared with microprobe and Hr ICP-MS) dictated the number of samples that I was able to submit. The primary criterion guiding my selection of sherds for INAA was to sample decorated and utility ware sherds from as many different contexts at each site as possible to maximize spatial and temporal representation. I submitted a larger proportion of St. Johns Polychrome and utility ware sherds to compensate for Duff's larger sample of Heshotauthla and Kwakina polychromes.

An additional sampling consideration was sherd size. The University of Missouri Research Reactor (MURR) archives a portion of each sherd that it analyzes, so I attempted to send them large sherds whenever possible. Because the INAA was conducted concurrently with the electron microprobe and lead isotope analyses, I was not able to take glaze paint composition into account (except at a very general level) when selecting my INAA sample of decorated ware. I selected utility ware sherds from the same excavation units as decorated sherds for each site. I attempted to avoid selecting multiple utility ware sherds from a single vessel by comparing paste color and surface treatment.

CERAMIC ASSEMBLAGE SERIATION

As with much of the Pueblo Southwest, ceramic seriation has a long history in the Zuni region (Duff 1996; Duff and Kintigh 1997; LeBlanc 1975, 1976, 1978; Marquardt 1974; Potter 1997). My recent seriation of ceramic collections (nearly all from excavated contexts) from El Morro Valley sites (Pueblo de los Muertos, Atsinna, Cienega, and Mirabal), and from Heshotauthla Pueblo and Box S Pueblo (Huntley 2004; Huntley and Kintigh 2004) resulted in the identification of sets of approximately contemporaneous assemblages within my larger ceramic sample. Since the seriation

Table 2.2. Date Ranges and Midpoints for Ceramic Types used in Seriation

Type	Date Range	Midpoint
Tularosa Black-on-white	A.D. 1175–1325	A.D. 1250
St. Johns Polychrome	A.D. 1200–1300	A.D. 1250
Springerville Polychrome	A.D. 1250–1300	A.D. 1275
Pinedale Polychrome	A.D. 1275–1375	A.D. 1325
Kwakina Polychrome*	A.D. 1275–1400	A.D. 1350
Heshotauthla Polychrome*	A.D. 1275–1400	A.D. 1350

*Dates for this type vary by source; I use Duff's (2002, Table 5.1) date ranges but a slightly later midpoint because production was likely most common from A.D. 1300–1400.

methodology is reported in detail in Huntley (2004) and Huntley and Kintigh (2004), I summarize the results here. I did not include Lower Pescado Village in the seriation due to slight differences in ceramic tabulation methods used by Rothschild and Dublin (1995), who did not distinguish or identify Springerville Polychrome and Pinedale Polychrome. I also excluded Spier 170 and Ojo Bonito from the seriation because these sites were not originally part of my research design and they were represented mainly by surface collections. I am, however, able to make general temporal assignments for the ceramic sample from these three sites, as discussed below.

Early and Late Ceramic Assemblages

Seriation was limited to six types that comprise the bulk of decorated ceramics at each of the nine sampled sites: Tularosa Black-on-white, St. Johns Polychrome, Pinedale Polychrome, Springerville Polychrome, Kwakina Polychrome, and Heshotauthla Polychrome. St. Johns Black-on-red and Heshotauthla Glaze-on-red are rare variants that are frequently indistinguishable from the polychrome types in sherd form. For the purposes of this analysis, the categories "St. Johns Polychrome" and "Heshotauthla Polychrome" include both identifiable polychrome and the black-on-red and glaze-on-red varieties. Date ranges (Table 2.2) for the occurrence of these types within the Zuni region have been published by Carlson (1970), Duff (1996, 2002), and Kintigh (1985a). The dates for Kwakina Polychrome and Heshotauthla Polychrome vary from source to source; in this analysis I use the dates published by Duff (2002, Table 5.1), which make the two types contemporaneous.

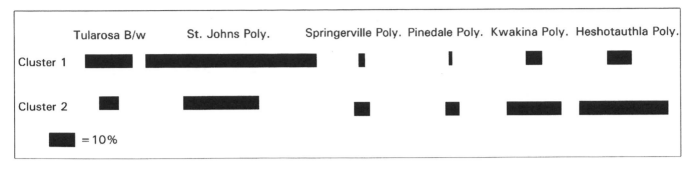

Figure 2.9. Ford diagram illustrating seriation of two clusters using six ceramic types.

I seriated 19,560 sherds in 123 analytical proveniences (individual or consolidated unit/level/locus collections) using a combination of correspondence analysis (CA), a multivariate scaling procedure (Baxter 1994; Bolviken and others 1982; Duff 1996), and k-means cluster analysis, a nonhierarchical procedure for grouping similar cases (Kintigh and Ammerman 1982).

The seriation highlights two clusters of ceramic analytical proveniences that represent early and late Pueblo IV components. The Ford diagram in Figure 2.9 graphically represents average percentages for each of the six ceramic types (Table 2.3) in chronological order for each cluster. St. Johns Polychrome and Tularosa Black-on-white dominate the early cluster (Cluster 1). Heshotauthla Polychrome, made beginning around A.D. 1275, dominates the late cluster (Cluster 2), and Kwakina Polychrome is also common. The relatively high percentages of St. Johns Polychrome and Tularosa Black-on-white in Cluster 2, however, are proportionately higher than might be expected for late assemblages, perhaps indicating that the very late end of the Pueblo IV period is underrepresented in the contexts I sampled.

Several additional lines of evidence help to establish relative dates for the two clusters. First, using South's (1978) mean ceramic date formula, I calculated an MCD of A.D. 1266 for Cluster 1 and an MCD of A.D. 1309 for Cluster 2 based on type midpoints in Table 2.2. The MCD for each cluster is calculated by multiplying the mean percentage of each ceramic type by the midpoint of that type's temporal range (Table 2.2) and dividing this value by the sum of the mean percentages (100%). The MCD calculation is intended as a general measure of the relative ages of each cluster and should be viewed with some caution because the result varies depending on the midpoints used for each type. Despite its potential shortcomings, the MCD calculation produces the right relative order for the two clusters. Moreover, tree-ring dates directly associated with sampled proveniences (Table 2.4) support a late 1200s date for Cluster 1. Unfortunately, few tree-ring dates are available, especially for Cluster 2. Finally, relative frequencies of glaze versus matte paints by cluster confirm my interpretation that the two clusters represent early and late components at each sampled site. In the White Mountain Red Ware sequence, it is clear that glaze paints

**Table 2.3. Ceramic Type Percentages and Descriptive Statistics
for Ceramic Assemblage Clusters**

Cluster	Tularosa Black/white	St. Johns Poly.	Springerville Poly.	Pinedale Poly.	Kwakina Poly.	Heshotauthla Poly.
1 (Early) n = 79						
Mean	17.7%	64.1%	2.1%	1.5%	5.9%	8.7%
Std. Dev.	9.6%	13.6%	2.3%	2.2%	4.3%	7.4%
2 (Late) n = 44						
Mean	6.8%	27.5%	6.2%	4.9%	21.1%	33.4%
Std. Dev.	4.9%	14.3%	5.5%	5.6%	10.9%	11.0%

NOTE: Shading indicates the most frequent types in each cluster.

Table 2.4. Tree-Ring Dates by K-means Cluster

Cluster	Cutting Dates	Latest Non-cutting Dates
1 (Early)	A.D. 1260; 1279; 1282; 1283; 1285; 1286; 1287; 1288	A.D. 1288; 1291
2 (Late)	A.D. 1284	A.D. 1286

Table 2.5. Early and Late Ceramic Analytical Provenience Frequencies by Site

Site	Early (Cluster 1) Count (Row %)		Late (Cluster 2) Count (Row %)		Total Count
Box S Pueblo	1	(100%)	-		1
Mirabal	13	(100%)	-		13
Pueblo de los Muertos	36	(65%)	19	(35%)	55
Heshotauthla	16	(62%)	10	(38%)	26
Cienega	9	(50%)	9	(50%)	18
Atsinna	4	(40%)	6	(60%)	10

gradually replaced matte paints on red-slipped types after about A.D. 1285 (Carlson 1970; Duff 1996; LeBlanc 1975, 1976; Marquardt 1974). The early and late clusters contain strikingly different ratios of matte (earlier) versus glaze (later) paints on St. Johns Polychrome and Heshotauthla Polychrome sherds. My glaze paint category includes both paints that appear (based on visual examination without magnification) to be fully vitrified, uniformly glassy paints, and variably glassy paints that were originally coded as "subglaze." In the early cluster (Cluster 1, n = 9,789) 66 percent of sherds have matte paint and 34 percent have glaze paints (a ratio of 2:1). In the late cluster (Cluster 2, n = 4,205), the percentage of sherds with matte paint drops to 28 percent and 72 percent of sherds have glaze paint (a ratio of 1:2.6).

Most sampled sites have both early and late ceramic analytical proveniences (Table 2.5). Box S Pueblo and Mirabal are exceptions. These two sites have only early ceramic assemblages and were most likely abandoned while other Zuni region settlements were still occupied, perhaps in the late 1200s or early 1300s (Kintigh 1985a; Watson and others 1980). The other four sites have contemporaneous early ceramic analytical proveniences in addition to late proveniences. In fact, Pueblo de los Muertos and Atsinna appear to contain some of the earliest proveniences in the seriation sample. Heshotauthla, Cienega, and Atsinna appear to have the largest proportions of late proveniences represented in the sample (Huntley 2004, Table A.1).

To summarize the seriation results, roughly contemporaneous ceramic analytical proveniences can be identified among the sampled sites. There is a marked clustering of early and late proveniences that makes sense in terms of previous chronologies for these sites, tree-ring dates, as well as relative frequencies of matte versus glaze paints. Based on the available evidence, I interpret the early cluster to represent archaeological contexts dating to the mid-to-late A.D. 1200s and the late

cluster to represent post-1300 contexts. Heshotauthla Pueblo, Atsinna, Pueblo de los Muertos, and Cienega have ceramics from both early and late contexts. Box S and Mirabal apparently have only early contexts. There is undoubtedly some overlap between early and late contexts, and finer chronological distinctions could be made. However, the seriation was intended to derive sets of approximately contemporaneous ceramic assemblages that can be used to assess temporal changes in pottery production and exchange within the Zuni region. The temporal assignments I have made are adequate for meeting this objective.

Lower Pescado Village, Spier 170, and Ojo Bonito Assemblages

Ceramic tabulations for Lower Pescado Village were compiled by Rothschild and Dublin (1995) as part of their investigations at this site. Lower Pescado Village was not included in my seriation because the ceramic tabulations for this site were completed by different researchers using slightly different typological attributes. The published ceramic tabulations do indicate general temporal assignments. The contexts I sampled at Lower Pescado Village typically contained low frequencies of St. Johns Polychrome and Tularosa Black-on-white sherds. Of the six decorated types included in my seriation, the largest proportion that Tularosa Black-on-white comprises of any sampled context from Lower Pescado Village is 8.3 percent (calculated using tabulations in Rothschild and Dublin 1995, Appendix J). This quantity is similar to the proportion of Tularosa Black-on-white in Cluster 2, which I have interpreted to represent relatively late archaeological contexts. Thus, the contexts that I sampled from Lower Pescado Village correspond reasonably well with later assemblages from the El Morro Valley and Heshotauthla Pueblo, and I include them with the late (post–A.D. 1300) group in subsequent chapters.

I did not include Spier 170 and Ojo Bonito in the seriation because ceramics from these two sites are primarily from surface collections. However, occupations at both pueblos are believed to post-date A.D. 1300 (Huntley and Kintigh 2004, Appendix; see also Chapter 1) and thus their ceramic assemblages are likely contemporaneous with the late assemblages from El Morro Valley and Heshotauthla Pueblo.

EXPECTATIONS FOR INTERACTION

The decorated ceramic types included in this research were innovative both in the use of glaze paints and the incorporation of a polychrome design scheme. They appear to have been widely produced and distributed within the Zuni region and nearby areas, such as the Upper Little Colorado River region, although there is little direct archaeological evidence of their manufacture and use. Studies of similar pottery types in other parts of the Southwest suggest that Pueblo IV glaze-decorated vessels were used in both domestic and ritual contexts. There is no archaeological evidence that craft specialists produced these vessels or that their use was restricted to Pueblo elites. Instead they were probably made and decorated by women within a household context.

In the chapters that follow, I use ceramic production and exchange data to examine interactions at several different scales. Interactions must have occurred on many different levels and involved both daily, face-to-face interactions encompassing households and kin groups, as well as more formal ritual, economic, and political transactions.

I interpret consistent selection of particular clays from a given set of available resources, similarities in glaze recipes, and similar use of color on ancestral Zuni vessels as indicative of close interactions at the pueblo or pueblo cluster level. Because glaze paint manufacture is something that presumably must be learned first-hand (or at least via word-of-mouth) rather than through imitation of a finished product (Herhahn 1995, 2006), use of particular glaze recipes may be attributed to the social framework in which a potter initially learned the technique. This aspect of glaze manufacture is best measured in the proportions of basic ingredients, such as the amount of lead ore added to produce a glassy finish

or the addition of a particular colorant to produce a desired color. Because consistently achieving a uniformly vitreous paint requires controlling a number of variables, including paint composition and firing temperature, atmosphere, and duration, potters were unlikely to dramatically alter particular production techniques once they had learned them. This does not exclude the possibility of innovation in glaze paint recipes, however, or the possibility that potters altered glaze recipes due to changes in resource availability.

The application of glaze paints and slips as decorative elements may reflect a conscious element of pottery manufacture. I am concerned with the extent to which potters from particular social groups (that is, pueblos or pueblo clusters) within the Zuni region used color or other decorative attributes to create visually distinctive ceramic vessels. Use of color might be related to contexts of use and participation in particular socioreligious systems.

Exchange of utility ware and decorated ware reflects the direction, intensity, and contexts of social interactions among residents of different pueblo clusters. Social relationships may have been affirmed through regularized exchanges of certain items, perhaps in the context of public ceremonies or social events. Glaze-decorated bowls are likely candidates for exchange in such contexts. Other researchers have presented convincing evidence that Rio Grande glaze-decorated bowls made during the Pueblo IV period were typically exchanged during the course of formal communal events (W. Graves 1996, 2002, 2004; Spielmann 1998). Assuming this is also true for the Zuni region, participants in public ceremonies, including visitors from other pueblos, may have supplied quantities of glaze-decorated bowls for use in the host pueblo. If decorated bowls used for multipueblo ceremonies remained at the host pueblo after use, there should be evidence for the movement of decorated vessels among nucleated pueblos with formal relationships. In contrast, utility ware was probably characterized by more informal exchanges among households or along kinship lines (Abbott 2000). As Zedeño (1998) suggests, relatively short-distance movement of utility ware also results from the permanent movement of people, such as the relocation of a household from one pueblo to another pueblo.

Use of glaze paints introduces the potential for interaction at the interregional level. Because the ores needed to make glaze paints are rare and, as shown in Chapter 5, were nonlocal, acquiring these materials would have required that individuals from the Zuni region establish certain social connections, regardless of whether ores were obtained via exchange or direct procurement.

In the case of exchange, individuals residing in the Zuni region would have had to maintain ties with distant groups to ensure a predictable supply of ore for glaze paint manufacture. In the case of direct procurement, travel to distant ore sources (historically done by groups of men) would have meant interacting with many different groups of people along the route, as well as residents of villages who may have exercised proprietary rights to local ore sources (Habicht-Mauche and others 2000).

CHAPTER THREE

Tracking Ceramic Production and Exchange Using INAA

As outlined in Chapter 2, previous studies of ceramic production and distribution based on compositional analysis indicate that pottery exchange among Zuni region nucleated pueblos was infrequent during the Pueblo IV period and earlier (Duff 1999, 2002; Stone 1992, 1994, 1999). My INAA characterization builds on these studies, with important refinements. A moderate amount of decorated pottery moved primarily from west to east within the Zuni region, a pattern that I interpret ·as an indicator of directional, formal interactions among residents of different pueblos. Utility ware, however, apparently moved much less often, suggesting informal exchanges among residents of different pueblo clusters, such as one might expect along kin lines, were relatively infrequent.

ZUNI REGIONAL GEOLOGY

Successful application of compositional analysis to tracking pottery production and distribution is predicated on a high level of geological diversity in the area under study. Although exposures of various geological formations overlap within the Zuni region, it is possible to distinguish general spatial differences in available clay resources. Duff (1999, 2002) and Mills (1995) present comprehensive maps and discussions of the distribution of clay resources within the Zuni region and the following summary is drawn in part from their work. The reader is also referred to Anderson (1987), Anderson and Maxwell (1991), Ferguson and Hart (1985), and the New Mexico Geological Society (1996) for more in-depth information on Zuni region geology.

The gradual decrease in elevation from northeast to southwest results in the exposure of different surface deposits in different portions of the Zuni region. On this basis, Duff (1999, 2002) subdivides the region into four major geological provinces, each with a distinctive geological setting. The easternmost province is the El Morro Valley, which is characterized by exposures of clay-bearing Dakota Sandstone deposits of Cretaceous age, Jurassic era Zuni Sandstone, and Triassic era Chinle Formation deposits (Fig. 3.1). In addition, Lower Permian deposits that underlie the entire Zuni region are exposed only on the eastern edge of the El Morro Valley (Anderson and Maxwell 1991; New Mexico Geological Society 1996). Clays from these deposits might have been available in alluvial contexts within the El Morro Valley (Duff 1999). Sampled pueblos in the Pescado Basin are within a zone of Cretaceous age Gallup Sandstone, but potters would also have had access to Dakota Formation, Mancos Shale, and Crevasse Canyon Formation materials (Anderson 1987; Mills 1995, Fig. 8.4; New Mexico Geological Society 1996). Potters at Box S Pueblo would have had access to a wide range of geological resources overlapping with the Pescado Basin and El Morro Valley.

In contrast to the eastern portion of the Zuni region, the Zuni River Basin contains extensive Chinle Formation deposits (Fig. 3.1; Mills 1995, Fig. 8.5). This area contained very little Pueblo IV occupation, however, and the current study includes no sites from this province. The Western province (Duff 1999, 2002) extends west from the Zuni Basin past the Arizona border and is geologically diverse, with exposures of Cretaceous Dakota Sandstone, Mancos Shale and Mesa Verde Sandstone, Triassic Chinle Formation deposits, and Tertiary Fence Lake and Bidahochi formations (Fig. 3.1). Pueblo IV potters in this province would have had easy access to both Dakota Sandstone and Mancos Shale clay-bearing deposits.

INAA

I selected samples of utility ware and decorated ware, as well as eight archaeological clay samples, for INAA. These samples came from a larger collection for which

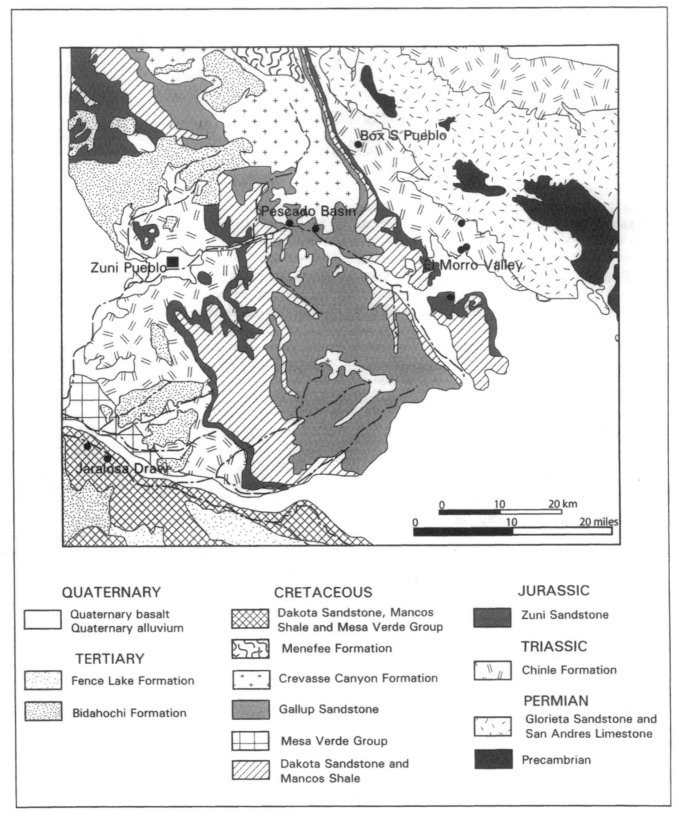

Figure 3.1. Locations of Zuni region clay formations in relation to sampled
sites (after Schachner 2007, Fig. 4.1; New Mexico Geological Society 1996).

Table 3.1. INAA Compositional Group Assignments for Samples by Site

Cluster/Site	Compositional Group (Count)					Unassigned	Total
	1	2a	2b	2c	4		
Atsinna	16	9	3	-	1	4 [1]	33
Cienega	13	3	2	-	-	4 [1]	22
Mirabal	9	5	2	5	-	1 [1]	22
Pueblo de los Muertos	14	12	3	-	-	7	36
El Morro Valley Subtotal	52	29	10	5	1 [2*]	16 [3]	113 [5]
Heshotauthla	-	26	4	-	-	6 [3]	36
Lower Pescado Village	1	26	4	-	-	4	35
Pescado Basin Subtotal	1	52	8	-	-	10 [3]	71 [3]
North Zuni region (Box S Pueblo)	-	11	3	13	-	3	30
Ojo Bonito	-	-	17	-	16 [1]	1 [5]	34
Spier 170	-	-	18	-	14 [2]	3 [3]	35
Southwest (Jaralosa Draw) Subtotal	-	-	35	-	30 [3]	4 [8]	69 [11]
Clays (from Barbara Mills)	-	-	-	-	-	[30]	[30]
Total	53	92	56	18	31 [5]	33 [44]	283 [49]

Note: Clay samples in brackets.
*Clay samples from El Morro Valley, precise provenience unknown.

I determined glaze paint compositions. Together with Duff's sample of 155 sherds and clays and Mills' data for 30 raw clays from the central Zuni region, my INAA dataset contained 332 individual cases (Huntley 2004, Table 4.1). Analysis of Duff's samples and my additional samples was performed at the Research Reactor at the University of Missouri, Columbia (MURR). Mills' clays were analyzed at the Conservation Analytical Lab (CAL) and were calibrated for comparability with the MURR data.

Methodology

INAA is predicated on the idea that archaeological ceramics and clays can be grouped according to similar chemical compositions, and that these compositional groups can be linked to production loci (Bishop and others 1982). INAA has been widely used in recent years to source archaeological ceramics from the American Southwest and elsewhere (Arnold and others 2000; Bishop and others 1988; Crown and Bishop 1991; Duff 1999, 2002; Glowacki and Neff 2002; Strazicich 1995; Triadan 1997). Duff (2002), Glascock (1992), Neff and Glowacki (2002) and Neff (2002a) provide detailed discussions of sample preparation, instrumentation, and the statistical procedures followed at MURR. I adhered as closely as possible to Duff's (1999, 2002) data reduction and statistical analysis methods (see also Huntley 2004, Chapter 5, for methodological details).

MURR researchers defined compositional groups in the collection and performed initial evaluations of the three largest groups (n > 32) using log-transformed elemental concentrations at MURR. I also used this method to assign a few originally unassigned samples to the large groups. I then used Mahalanobis distance-based probabilities based on 16 principal components to evaluate smaller groups and to assign several previously unassigned samples to the original MURR groups (Huntley 2004, Tables B.1–B.6 contain raw data and supporting statistics).

Compositional Groups

Of the total INAA dataset, 250 sherds and 5 clay samples were assigned to five compositional groups (Table 3.1) that generally correspond to groups defined previously by Duff (1999, 2002). MURR originally defined an additional group (Group 3) that had only three members. I was able to assign one sample from this group to another group; the other two remained unassigned. Ten percent of the collection (33 sherds) and the majority of clay samples (n = 44 of 49; 13% of

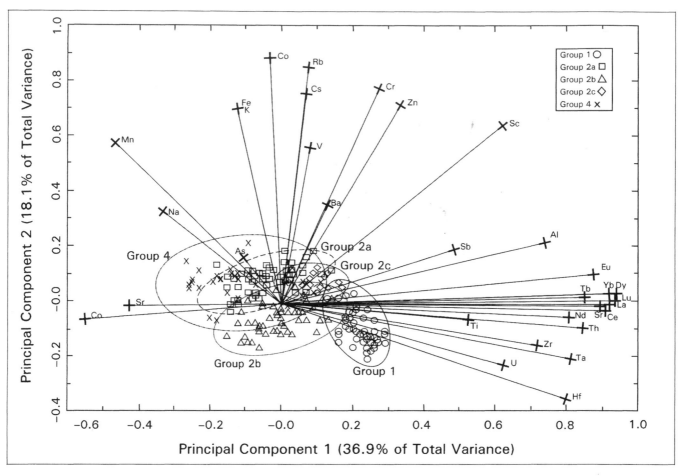

Figure 3.2. All compositional groups plotted by principal components 1 and 2 (with 95% confidence ellipses).

the 332 cases) cannot confidently be assigned to a compositional group and are considered unclassified (Huntley 2004, Tables B.4 and B.6). This percentage of unassigned samples is not unusual for compositional datasets, which typically contain 30 percent or more unclassified specimens (Duff 2002; Neff and Glowacki 2002). Figure 3.2, an RQ-mode plot that simultaneously projects samples (within 95% confidence ellipses for each group) and variables, shows samples plotted by factor scores based on principal components 1 and 2. Unassigned samples are not included in this or subsequent plots for clarity of data presentation.

As Figure 3.2 indicates, Group 1 is characterized by high rare earth element (REE) concentrations on the lower right side of the plot. Fifty-two of fifty-three samples assigned to this group came from various El Morro Valley sites (Table 3.1). A single utility ware sherd from Lower Pescado Village is also in this group. Group 1 contains slightly more utility ware than deco-

rated ware (Table 3.2). Of the decorated types classified in Group 1, Heshotauthla Polychrome is most common (n = 13). Group 1 samples represent both early and late archaeological contexts (as defined in Chapter 2) from sampled sites, with samples from late contexts more than twice as common (Table 3.3).

Compositional Groups 2a, 2b, and 2c appear to represent partitions of a compositional continuum (Fig. 3.2). Groups 2a and 2b have lower REE concentrations than Group 1 and can be distinguished from one another based on tantalum versus ytterbium concentrations (Fig. 3.3). Most of the samples (52 of 92) in Group 2a are from Heshotauthla Pueblo and Lower Pescado Village, with smaller numbers of samples from the El Morro Valley (n = 29) and Box S Pueblo (n = 11; Table 3.1). Group 2a equates reasonably well with Duff's EAST group (Huntley 2004, Table B.2), which he argues represents use of clay resources from the Dakota Sandstone Formation by some El Morro Valley and

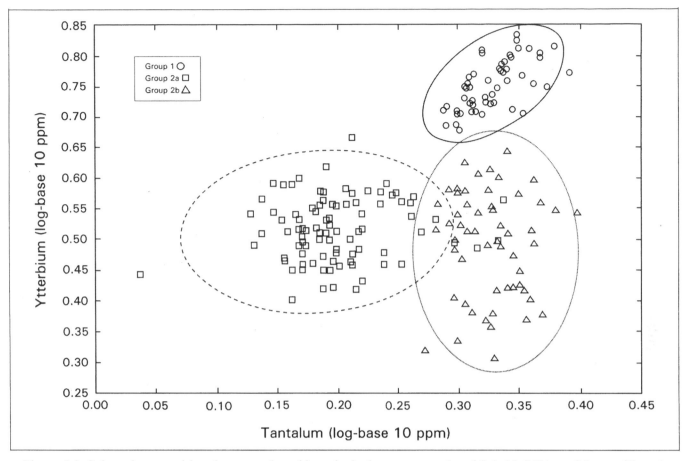

Figure 3.3. Selected compositional groups plotted by principal components 1 and 3 (with 95% confidence ellipses).

Table 3.2. Ceramic Type Frequencies by Compositional Group (All Sites Combined)

Cluster/Site	Compositional Group (Count)					Unassigned	*Total*
	1	2a	2b	2c	4		
St. Johns Polychrome	5	11	8	9	-	6	*39*
Heshotauthla Polychrome	13	44	18	1	5	7	*88*
Kwakina Polychrome	4	22	15	5	5	6	*57*
Other Glaze Types*	1	-	5	-	3	-	*9*
Decorated Ware Subtotal	*23*	*77*	*46*	*15*	*13*	*19*	*193*
Utility Ware	30	15	10	3	18	14	*90*
Total	*53*	*92*	*56*	*18*	*31*	*33*	*283*

*6 Pinnawa Glaze-on-white, 1 Pinnawa Red-on-white, and 2 Kechipawan Polychrome sherds analyzed by Duff (1999).

Table 3.3. Relatively Early and Late Samples by Compositional Group

Time Period	Compositional Group										*Total*	
	1		2a		2b		2c		4			
	Count	(Col. %)	Count	(Col. %)	Count	(Col. %)	Count	(Col. %)	Count	(Col. %)	*Count*	*(Col. %)*
Early	16	(33%)	33	(37%)	9	(21%)	18	(100%)	1	(6%)	*77*	*(35%)*
Late	33	(67%)	57	(63%)	35	(79%)	-		17	(94%)	*142*	*(65%)*
Total	*49*	*(100%)*	*90*	*(100%)*	*44*	*(100%)*	*18*	*(100%)*	*18*	*(100%)*	*219*	*(100%)*

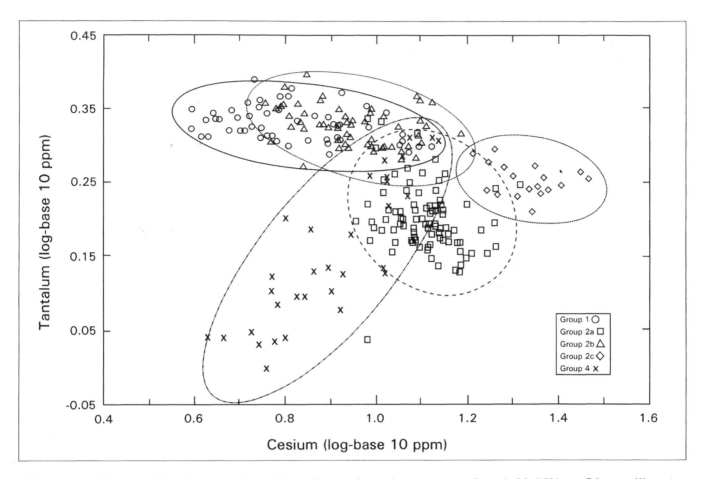

Figure 3.4. All compositional groups plotted by cesium and tantalum concentrations (with 95% confidence ellipses).

Heshotauthla potters (Duff 2002: 134). Group 2a also contains a large proportion of decorated ware relative to utility ware (n = 77, 83.7% of the samples in this group), the majority of which are Heshotauthla Polychrome sherds (Table 3.2). Almost two-thirds of the samples in this group are from late archaeological contexts at sampled sites (Table 3.3).

Group 2b is dominated by Duff's samples from Ojo Bonito and Spier 170 (Table 3.1); 35 of 56 sherds in Group 2b came from these two sites (10 were from the El Morro Valley, 8 were from the Pescado Basin, and 3 were from Box S Pueblo). Duff (1999, 2002) classified most of these samples in Group OB1, which he attributes to production in the southwestern part of the Zuni region, possibly using Mancos Shale clays. However, based on the compositional similarity of Group 2b to Groups 2a and 2c, Group 2b might alternatively be attributed to Dakota Sandstone Formation clays in the southwestern Zuni region. Like Group 2a, Group 2b contains a large number of decorated ware sherds (n =

46, 82.1% of all samples in this group) compared with utility ware (Table 3.2). Samples from late archaeological contexts comprise the majority of samples in this group (Table 3.3), reflecting the overall late dates of Ojo Bonito and Spier 170.

A cesium-tantalum plot (Fig. 3.4) shows the distinction between Group 2c and Groups 2a and 2b. Group 2c is comprised of samples from early archaeological contexts mainly from Box S Pueblo (13 of 18 samples in this group; Tables 3.1 and 3.3) and includes five samples from Mirabal in the El Morro Valley. Since sherds from Box S are most common in Group 2c, vessels in this group may have been made from clays at the northern end of the Dakota Sandstone in the vicinity of this pueblo. As in Groups 2a and 2b, decorated ware is more common (15 of 18 samples) in Group 2c than utility ware (Table 3.2). St. Johns Polychrome is the most common decorated type present in this group (n = 9).

Group 4 is unusual in that it is characterized by low thorium and high manganese concentrations (Fig. 3.1).

This chemically diverse group is dominated by 30 sherds and 3 raw clay samples from Ojo Bonito and Spier 170 (Table 3.1). Samples are overwhelmingly from late archaeological contexts (Table 3.3). Group 4 generally corresponds with Duff's (2002) group OB2, which he attributes to the western Zuni area. Based on the fact that two raw clays collected in the El Morro Valley fit this group's compositional profile, it may represent a class of raw materials (perhaps alluvial clays) available across much of the Zuni region. Unfortunately, the exact proveniences and geological contexts of the clay samples from the El Morro Valley in Group 4 are unknown. An alternative explanation is that the similarity between the two El Morro clay samples and ceramics from Ojo Bonito and Spier 170 is spurious. This possibility seems likely considering the overall lack of ceramic samples from El Morro Valley sites in Group 4 and that the three additional clay samples from archaeological contexts at El Morro Valley sites cannot be assigned to Group 4. Even if they are similar to clay resources available in the southwestern portion of the Zuni region, the two unprovenienced El Morro Valley clays do not appear to have been utilized by El Morro Valley potters.

Notably, nearly all of the clay samples (n = 44, 89.8%) are considered unassigned. The majority of raw clays (30 samples collected by Mills) are unprepared geological clays from Dakota Sandstone and Chinle Formation deposits located along the Zuni River drainage in the central portion of the Zuni reservation (Fig. 3.1). There was limited Pueblo IV occupation in this area, and it is not surprising that these clays do not correspond well with the ceramic sample. It is also possible that the unprepared clays recovered from archaeological contexts at Heshotauthla Pueblo and El Morro Valley sites were intended for use as construction materials and not as pottery clays.

It seems unlikely that pottery made from archaeological clays is absent in the INAA samples from these sites. A more likely explanation is that the lack of fit between clay samples and ceramic sherds is the result of adding temper during the vessel manufacturing process. Temper can have a substantial effect on overall chemical composition (Neff and Glowacki 2002), and raw, untempered clays may be difficult to match chemically with sherds from tempered vessels. Mills and her colleagues (Mills and others 1999) report this problem in their compositional analysis of clay samples from the Silver Creek area. None of the geological clay samples

Table 3.4. Number of Samples in Each Compositional Group (Excluding Unknowns) by Cluster

	Production Source Area/Group (Count)					
	El Morro Valley	Pescado	North	Southwest		
Cluster	1	2a	2c	2b	4	*Total*
El Morro Valley	52	<u>29</u>	<u>5</u>	<u>10</u>	<u>1</u>	*97*
Pescado	<u>1</u>	52	-	<u>8</u>	-	*61*
North	-	<u>11</u>	13	<u>3</u>	-	*27*
Southwest	-	-	-	35	30	*65*
Total	*53*	*92*	*18*	*56*	*31*	*250*

NOTE: This table does not include clay samples. Underlining indicates nonlocal sherds.

they analyzed could be matched with their sherd compositional groups. With a larger sample size and mineralogical analysis of Zuni region ceramics it might be possible to model the effects of different temper additions on raw clay compositions.

To summarize, the five INAA compositional groups correspond to the four regional geological subdivisions defined by Duff (1999, 2002; Fig. 3.1). As indicated in Table 3.4, 54 percent (n = 52) of all sherds from El Morro Valley sites (n = 97) are classified in compositional Group 1, 85 percent (n = 52) of samples from Heshotauthla Pueblo and Lower Pescado Village in the Pescado Basin (n = 61) are in Group 2a, and all samples from the sites of Ojo Bonito and Spier 170 (n = 65) are in Groups 2b and 4. Samples from Box S Pueblo are slightly more common in Group 2c (n = 13; 48%) than in Group 2a (n = 11; 41%). Based on the criterion of abundance, compositional Group 1 appears to correspond to the El Morro Valley, compositional Group 2a to the Pescado Basin (with perhaps some overlap with the El Morro Valley), and Groups 2b and 4 to the far southwestern portion of the Zuni region. Group 2c is unique in that all samples in this group come from early archaeological contexts, and this group likely corresponds to the northern Zuni region where Box S Pueblo is located.

INTRAREGIONAL EXCHANGE

The INAA results reveal that potters tended to use locally available clay resources for both decorated and utility ware, evidence that potters' communities of practice were mainly defined at the pueblo or pueblo cluster level. It also appears that some ceramic exchange occurred among pueblo clusters located in different geological clay resource areas (production zones), and that the majority of exchanged pottery moved from west to east within the Zuni region. The pottery sample from the El Morro Valley pueblo cluster, in particular, contains a higher proportion of nonlocal vessels, especially decorated ware, than do the samples from the Pescado Basin cluster, Box S Pueblo, and two pueblos in the southwestern Zuni region. Importantly, my ability to detect exchange within the region is determined by the scale at which I can distinguish clay sources. In other words, I can detect ceramic exchanges among nucleated pueblos located in different production zones, but I cannot detect exchanges among nucleated pueblos within the same production zone. For example, because Heshotauthla Pueblo and Lower Pescado Village probably used similar clay sources within a relatively small portion of the Pescado Basin (or perhaps even the same source), we cannot track pottery exchange between these two pueblos.

There are several reasons why sites in the El Morro Valley, the Pescado Basin, and the northern portion of the Zuni region contain sherds from multiple production zones. One possible explanation is that clay resources within different production zones may be compositionally distinct from one another, but potters may have exploited clay resources from multiple production zones. This scenario may be possible for pueblos located in the Pescado Basin, Box S, and the El Morro Valley, whose residents would have had access to a variety of northwest to southeast-trending geological formations (Fig. 3.1). If potters used a variety of clays indiscriminately, however, I would not expect to see such strong geographical patterning of INAA compositional groups. Moreover, cross-cultural studies have shown that potters typically travel no more than 7 km to 8 km (4–5 miles) to obtain clay resources (Arnold 1985), making it likely that potters in particular pueblo clusters consistently selected from a limited range of locally available clays.

Another possibility, which is plausible if we accept the premise that chemically distinct clay resource zones correspond generally to the spatial distribution of pueblo clusters, is that the presence of samples from multiple production zones at some nucleated pueblos is the result of intercluster exchange. Assuming this is the case, then 68 sherds (27% of the assigned sample) were found outside of the production area in which they were made. This proportion is higher than that reported by Duff (1999, 2002), who interprets approximately 8 percent nonlocal sherds in his Zuni region INAA sample as indicative of low-level exchange. It is lower, however, than reported nonlocal ceramic frequencies for many other thirteenth and fourteenth century Southwestern ceramic assemblages. Zedeño (1994: 107) reports that at least one-third of both decorated and utility ware was imported to Chodistaas Pueblo, and Triadan (1997, Table 4.5) demonstrates that 40 to 50 percent of White Mountain Red Ware was imported to Grasshopper Pueblo. Thus, I characterize the frequency of ceramic exchange within the Zuni region as moderate at best.

As indicated in Figure 3.5, which shows the distribution of sherds from the four production zones aggregated by pueblo cluster, it appears that ceramics primarily moved from west to east within the Zuni region. Sherds from the southwestern production zone comprise between 11 percent and 13 percent of the INAA samples from the Pescado Basin, North Zuni region, and El Morro Valley. However, no sherds from these three areas were identified in the ceramic sample from Ojo Bonito and Spier 170 (Southwest zone). Sherds attributed to the Pescado Basin production zone make up 41 percent of the INAA sample from Box S Pueblo (North zone) and 30 percent of the El Morro Valley sample. This pattern may be due, at least in part, to shared resources among these three areas. A small number of sherds probably produced in the area north of the Pescado Basin are also found at El Morro Valley sites (n = 5; 5% of the El Morro Valley INAA sample). Although the El Morro Valley cluster seems to have received ceramics from throughout the Zuni region, pottery from the El Morro Valley production zone is conspicuously absent at sites outside of the El Morro Valley. A single sherd attributed to the El Morro Valley production zone is present in the INAA sample from Lower Pescado Village in the Pescado Basin (Table 3.1).

Calculation of Brainerd-Robinson similarity coefficients (Shennan 1997: 233) statistically evaluates apparent intersite and intercluster differences in the distributions of ceramics from different compositional groups, which I equate with production zones. Brainerd-Robinson coefficients for site assemblages are in Table 3.5 and for combined cluster assemblages in Table 3.6.

Using the combined proportions of all of the production zones as the population, I can calculate the proba-

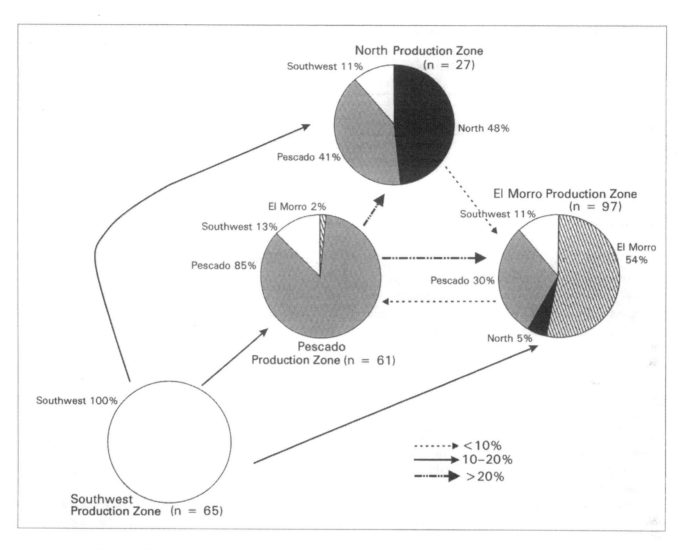

Figure 3.5. Distribution of compositional groups among production zones/pueblo clusters.

Table 3.5. Brainerd-Robinson Similarity Coefficients for Intracluster and Intercluster (in italics) Comparisons of Sample Percentages from Different Sites

Site	Atsinna	Cienega	Mirabal	Pueblo de los Muertos	Hesho-tauthla	Lower Pescado Village	Box S	Ojo Bonito	Spier 170
Atsinna	-								
Cienega	168	-							
Mirabal	155	137	-						
Pueblo de los Muertos	173	159	150	-					
Heshotauthla	*96*	*80*	*73*	*117*	-				
Lower Pescado Village	*101*	*75*	*80*	*112*	189	-			
Box S	*92*	*66*	*119*	*103*	*114*	*115*	-		
Ojo Bonito	*26*	*20*	*39*	*19*	*24*	*25*	*22*	-	
Spier 170	*42*	*36*	*27*	*35*	*40*	*41*	*38*	182	-

Table 3.6. Brainerd-Robinson Similarity Coefficients for Intracluster and Intercluster (in italics) Comparisons of Sample Percentages from Different Production Zones

Production Zone	El Morro Valley	Pescado	North	Southwest
El Morro Valley	165			
Pescado	*103*	189		
North	*100*	*115*	-	
Southwest	*32*	*35*	*31*	182

bility of obtaining by chance, from this population, two samples as different as, or even more different than, the two samples I am comparing. I performed the calculation for every available pair of samples using the BRSAMPLE program available in Kintigh's (2002) *Tools for Quantitative Archaeology* to calculate probabilities. This program incorporates a Monte Carlo simulation that repeatedly draws samples with specified sizes with replacement from a given population with given type proportions. The proportion of Monte Carlo trials with a coefficient $< = $ K provides a measure of the probability of obtaining by chance a similarity of K or less between two given samples (Kintigh 2002: 80). I can then evaluate whether the observed variability is a result of sampling error, considering the relatively small sample sizes from each site. A cumulative probability of 0.50 associated with a coefficient of 180 indicates that I would obtain a coefficient of 180 or less 50 percent of the time simply by chance. Thus, for comparisons among the site and cluster samples listed in Tables 3.5 and 3.6, relatively high coefficients indicate that differences among sites in their proportions of samples from different production zones are not behaviorally meaningful and can be attributed to sample error. Conversely, I interpret relatively low coefficients to indicate significant differences among sites in the proportions of samples from different production zones.

Settlements located in different pueblo clusters have low Brainerd-Robinson coefficients and very low probabilities of obtaining coefficients equal to or less than the calculated values for each pair of settlement assemblages, suggesting that differences between them are not likely attributable to chance. For the Pueblo de los Muertos and Heshotauthla assemblages, for example, the probability of obtaining such dissimilar samples

by chance is .003, or .3 percent. I obtained even lower probabilities for comparisons among many other settlements from different pueblo clusters, suggesting that the observed intercluster differences in production zone proportions are not attributable to sampling error. On the other hand, settlements located within the same pueblo cluster have high coefficients and high probabilities, suggesting that small differences among them might be attributable to chance due to sampling error. Sample assemblages are not really a random sample of the global population of production source groups. However, the coefficients and probabilities are sufficiently high (within cluster differences) or low (intercluster differences) to indicate that settlements within the same cluster have similar production sources and settlements in different clusters have different production sources. Thus, it is not necessary to perform chi-square or other statistical tests to evaluate these differences.

Although I do not have the compositional resolution to evaluate ceramic circulation within pueblo clusters, I can say with some certainty that settlements within clusters appear to have had remarkably similar distributions of pottery from different production zones. In the El Morro Valley, Pueblo de los Muertos and Atsinna have the largest proportion of sherds from production zones other than the El Morro Valley zone (15 of 36 sherds and 13 of 33 sherds, respectively, see Table 3.1), but their samples are similar overall to the samples from Cienega and Mirabal. Mirabal's INAA sample is different from the other three El Morro Valley pueblo samples, and I attribute at least some of this difference to time, because Mirabal likely has an early assemblage (Chapter 2). Within the Pescado cluster, Heshotauthla Pueblo and Lower Pescado Village samples have equal numbers of presumably local (n = 26) and nonlocal (n = 4) ceramics. Notably, Spier 170 and Ojo Bonito (representing the Jaralosa Draw cluster) have no imported ceramics.

There also are apparent differences in production and exchange of utility ware and various decorated types. Table 3.7 presents, by pueblo cluster, the percentages of sherds of each type that appear to be of nonlocal origin, excluding unassigned samples. Of the 68 sherds presumably recovered from outside their production zone, Heshotauthla Polychrome comprises the largest proportion (n = 27; 40% of all nonlocal sherds), followed by St. Johns Polychrome (n = 16; 24% of all nonlocal sherds), utility ware (n = 15; 22% of all nonlocal

Table 3.7. Percentages of Presumed Nonlocal Pottery by Ceramic Type for Each Cluster

Ceramic Type (n = INAA sample total)	Pueblo Cluster				
	El Morro Count (Row %)	Pescado Count (Row %)	North Count (Row %)	Southwest Count (Row %)	*Nonlocal Total Count* (% of Type)
St. Johns Poly. (n = 33)	11 of 16 (69%)	2 of 6 (33%)	3 of 11 (27%)	-	*16 of 33* (48%)
Heshotauthla Poly. (n = 69)	21 of 34 (62%)	2 of 23 (9%)	4 of 5 (80%)	0 of 7 (0%)	*27 of 69* (39%)
Kwakina Poly. (n = 43)	10 of 14 (71%)	0 of 17 (0%)	0 of 1 (0%)	0 of 11 (0%)	*10 of 43* (23%)
Utility Ware (n = 73)	3 of 31 (9%)	5 of 14 (33%)	7 of 10 (70%)	0 of 18 (0%)	*15 of 73* (21%)
Total (n = 218)	*45 of 95* (43%)	*9 of 60* (15%)	*14 of 27* (52%)	*0 of 36* (0%)	*68 of 218* (31%)

NOTE: Clay samples and 9 protohistoric Zuni Glaze Ware sherds are excluded from this table, as are samples from unknown sources (n = 33).

sherds), and Kwakina Polychrome (n = 10; 15% of all nonlocal sherds). Taking individual type sample sizes into account, however, reveals that nearly half (n = 16) of the 33 sampled St. Johns Polychrome sherds that can be attributed to source are presumed nonlocal (that is, they were discarded outside of their presumed production zone). For Heshotauthla Polychrome, 27 of 69 sampled sherds (39%) are presumed nonlocal, 10 of 43 (23%) of Kwakina Polychrome sherds are presumed nonlocal, and 15 of 73 (21%) utility ware sherds are presumed nonlocal. This would imply that red-slipped wares, particularly early St. Johns Polychrome, were more widely traded within the region, whereas Kwakina Polychrome and utility wares were less frequently exchanged.

Table 3.7 also highlights greater frequencies of nonlocal decorated ware at El Morro Valley pueblos than elsewhere in the Zuni region. Sixty-nine percent (11 of 16) of all St. Johns Polychrome sherds in the El Morro Valley sample of 95 sourced sherds are presumed nonlocal. The percentages of nonlocal Heshotauthla Polychrome (62%; 21 of 34 sherds in the El Morro Valley sample) and Kwakina Polychrome (71%; 10 of 14 sherds in the El Morro Valley sample) are similarly high. Furthermore, it appears that only sites in the El Morro Valley have nonlocal Kwakina Polychrome in their assemblages. These nonlocal Kwakina vessels came from several different production zones: five sherds from the Pescado Basin, one from the North zone, four from the Southwest zone, and four from an unknown source or sources. El Morro Valley sites also have a much smaller proportion of nonlocal utility ware pottery (9%; 3 of 31 total El Morro Valley utility sherds) compared with the Pescado Basin (36%; 5 of 14

total utility sherds in the Pescado Basin sample) and Box S (70%; 7 of 10 utility sherds in the North sample).

Because the percentages of nonlocal decorated ware versus nonlocal utility ware within my sample appear different among some of the sampled sites, it is important to consider the potential effects of different overall assemblage sizes on the actual numbers of nonlocal vessels. At a given site, for example, if there is twice as much utility ware overall compared with decorated ware, then five percent of utility ware represents the same number of vessels as ten percent of decorated ware. In this case, the actual numbers of nonlocal utility and decorated vessels are the same despite different proportions.

Fisher's Exact test is an alternative to the chi-square statistic for comparing differences among groups with small or disproportionate sample sizes. For a given 2x2 contingency table, Fisher's Exact test computes the exact probability of obtaining random observations as extreme, or more extreme, than the observed cell frequencies if the variables being examined truly are independent (Thomas 1986: 291). A lower probability indicates that it is unlikely that a result as extreme or more extreme than the observed result could occur at random. I used the FISHER program available in Kintingh's (2002) *Tools for Quantitative Archaeology* to compute probabilities, which should not be viewed as strict tests of significance. Rather, they evaluate how reasonable it is to draw conclusions regarding the similarity or differences between two groups.

A Fisher's Exact test on the distribution of all nonlocal decorated ware versus nonlocal utility ware in the El Morro Valley cluster versus the Pescado Basin cluster produces a two-tailed probability of 0.002. The two-tailed probability for the El Morro Valley cluster versus Box S is even lower (0.001). Thus, I conclude that the El Morro Valley cluster has a significantly higher proportion of nonlocal decorated ware compared with the Pescado Basin cluster and Box S Pueblo. Although differences among most El Morro Valley sites and Box S Pueblo might be explained, at least in part, by differences in the relative dates of their sampled assemblages, such is not the case for the largely contemporaneous Pescado Basin sites.

INTERPRETATIONS

Previous studies indicate that ceramic exchange within the Zuni region was uncommon during the Pueblo IV period. Stone's (1992) analysis suggests that the roots of this pattern extend back to the mid–A.D. 1100s or earlier. Ceramic exchange appears to have become more prevalent after 1400, as suggested by Mills' (1995) analysis of protohistoric Zuni glaze-decorated vessels from the Zuni River Basin. Community specialization in the production of glaze-decorated vessels appears to have developed after about A.D. 1400, a situation for which we have no evidence during earlier time periods. The current INAA partitioned decorated and utility ware sherds and raw clays from the Zuni region into five compositional groups that apparently represent four production zones, each with geologically distinctive clay resources. It appears that potters within these production zones consistently selected clay resources nearest to the pueblo (or pueblo cluster) in which they resided. Thus, ceramic paste compositions reflect potting communities of practice defined at the pueblo or pueblo cluster level, as might be expected based on cross-cultural studies of clay resource procurement (Arnold 1985).

Comparison of the distributions of sherds from each production zone among pueblo clusters indicates that exchange was more common among some clusters than others, with nonlocal ceramics accounting for around one-fourth of the total INAA sample. This proportion is substantially larger than that reported by Duff (1999, 2002) and Stone (1992, 1994, 1999), but still does not approach the scale of community-level specialized production and distribution systems found in the Hopi area (Bernardini 2005; Bishop and others 1988) or in the Rio Grande Valley (W. Graves and Spielmann 2000; Nelson and Habicht-Mauche 2006; Shepard 1942; Warren 1981).

It is noteworthy that St. Johns Polychrome and Heshotauthla Polychrome vessels were most commonly exchanged among pueblo clusters and that Kwakina Polychrome vessels were rarely exchanged. Only El Morro Valley sites have nonlocal Kwakina Polychrome vessels. This is curious in light of the observation that some Zuni region sites contain greater frequencies of Kwakina Polychrome than others (Chapter 2). In particular, Heshotauthla Pueblo contains more Kwakina Polychrome in later assemblages than do El Morro Valley sites, and it is possible that Heshotauthla potters stepped up production of this type for exchange to El Morro Valley pueblos during the mid to late 1300s.

Based on overall lower levels of utility ware exchange within the region, I proposed that informal social transactions among residents of different pueblo clusters were irregular, or at least did not regularly involve ceramic exchange. This pattern was not universal, however, as some utility ware was exchanged. Comparatively large proportions of nonlocal utility ware in the Pescado Basin and the Box S area, for example, could have resulted from more informal intercluster interactions between these two areas.

Significantly, there clearly is a west to east directional component to decorated ceramic exchange within the Zuni region. Nucleated pueblos in the El Morro Valley have more nonlocal ceramics than pueblos in other clusters, but sherds attributed to the El Morro Valley production area are virtually absent in the ceramic samples from clusters located farther west. The pueblos of Ojo Bonito and Spier 170, located in the far southwestern portion of the Zuni region, appear to have exchanged ceramics with pueblos located in the eastern half of the Zuni region, but apparently did not receive ceramics in return. Based on this pattern, I argue that El Morro Valley residents engaged in social interactions that resulted in the exchange of pottery to them, but that the exchange was not in kind. Since exchange implies a two-way transaction, something else must have been given in return. One explanation for this pattern is that El Morro Valley residents, as relative newcomers to the Zuni region, attempted to negotiate social alliances with their neighbors elsewhere in the Zuni region via formal exchanges within the larger context of integrative rituals. Such integrative rituals might have attracted populations from other pueblo clusters, who brought with them decorated bowls that eventually made their way into El Morro Valley pottery assemblages. In return, they may have obtained food and other material goods, or received less tangible returns such as esoteric information and opportunities to fulfill social obligations.

In summary, this INAA of ceramic pastes shows that nucleated pueblos located in different parts of the Zuni region consistently utilized chemically distinguishable clay sources to make both decorated and utility ware vessels. My analysis indicates that ceramic exchange was not pervasive within the Pueblo IV Zuni region and involved mainly decorated ware that primarily moved from west to east in the Zuni region, especially into the El Morro Valley, whereas nonlocal utility ware was more common in the Pescado Basin and at Box S Pueblo. I speculate that informal intercluster interactions resulted in the movement of utility ware into these last two areas and that multipueblo integrative rituals facilitated movement of decorated ware into the El Morro Valley.

CHAPTER FOUR

Glaze Recipes, Use of Color, and Patterns of Regional Interaction

During the late thirteenth century, potters in the Zuni region and elsewhere in the Pueblo Southwest began using glaze paints to decorate their pottery. Use of glaze paint represented a major technological innovation, because the relatively low firing temperatures used by Pueblo potters meant well-vitrified glazes could only be achieved by formulating certain combinations of ingredients. Early experiments with vitreous paints are known from the Four Corners region (Hawley 1929) and west Mexico (Weigand 1975), but neither of these examples matches the temporal or spatial extent of Pueblo glaze technology (see Eckert 2006 for a review).

My analysis of glaze paint compositions on St. Johns Polychrome and ancestral Zuni glaze-decorated vessels indicates a shift in basic glaze recipes through time, from heterogeneous, low lead/high copper glazes to homogeneous, high lead/low copper glazes. Although the compositional data point to temporal variability in the adoption of a high lead recipe, there is no evidence for distinctive pueblo or pueblo cluster glaze recipes indicative of cohesive communities of practice at this scale, nor is there strong patterning in the use of certain glaze colors by particular pueblos or pueblo clusters. Zuni region potters apparently interacted with one another often enough to share technological and stylistic information concerning glaze manufacture.

Regional patterns in exterior and interior bowl slip colors indicate fairly consistent use of particular red hues on entirely red-slipped bowls (St. Johns Polychrome and Heshotauthla Polychrome), but minor intercluster differences in the use of white hues on Kwakina Polychrome bowl interiors. This pattern may be attributed partly to intraregional slip clay distributions, but it also implies the presence of widely held conventions concerning the use of background colors that may relate to different use contexts for St. Johns and Heshotauthla vessels versus Kwakina Polychrome.

PUEBLO GLAZE TECHNOLOGY

The conventional wisdom concerning Pueblo glaze technology is that in order to produce a paint that vitrifies on firing, detailed technical knowledge and careful manipulation of raw materials and firing practices was necessary (Carlson 1970; De Atley 1986; Habicht-Mauche 1993; Snow 1982). A glaze is a glass formed when particular combinations of minerals vitrify during exposure to heat (Rhodes 1973). Silica is the crucial ingredient present in all glazes. Other materials, known as fluxes, are necessary to lower the melting point of silica. Lead is one of the best fluxes for low-fired glazes. It can lower the vitrification point of a glaze to around 700° C, which would have been obtainable by Pueblo potters (Shepard 1956). Alumina is also required to prevent the melted glaze from becoming too thin. The addition of small amounts of particular colorants such as iron, manganese, and copper to lead-silica glazes allows the potter to produce a wide range of glaze colors (Rhodes 1973).

Previous compositional analyses of Pueblo glaze paints have identified regionally distinctive glaze compositions (Bower and others 1986; De Atley 1986; Fenn and others 2006; Hawley 1938; Herhahn 2006; Huntley and Herhahn 1996; Huntley and others 2007; Shepard 1942, 1965) and demonstrated that distinct glaze recipes can be identified within individual archaeological sites (De Atley 1986; Huntley 1997; Jones 1995). The earliest analysis of Western Pueblo glazes was undertaken by Fred Hawley (1938), who reported moderate to high copper concentrations and low to moderate lead concentrations in St. Johns Polychrome, Pinedale Polychrome, and Fourmile Polychrome glazes he examined. Anna Shepard (1942, 1965) performed pioneering basic chemical studies of Rio Grande glazes produced during the fourteenth through sixteenth centuries A.D. She found the main ingredients of Rio Grande glazes to be consistent through time, although the amount of lead present increased from 20–30 percent to 50–60 percent (Shepard 1942: 222). Shepard argued that this change would account for the greater degree of vitrification (glass formation) observed in later Rio Grande glazes and speculated that Rio Grande potters compounded several raw materials to produce specific glaze mixtures. Shepard (1942: 222) also analyzed several Fourmile and Pinedale glazes and reported high copper and silica in these types compared with the Rio Grande glazes. Her analysis led her to conclude that two entirely different kinds of ore were the primary ingredients for the high lead glazes of the Rio Grande versus the high copper and silica glazes of east-central Arizona. The two Heshotauthla Polychrome glazes that she analyzed were different from one another in terms of lead and copper concentrations, suggesting that potters who made these vessels used either high lead or high copper recipes. Suzanne De Atley (1986) identified three distinct glaze compositional groups within a sample of fourteenth century White Mountain Red Ware from Fourmile Ruin in east-central Arizona. These compositional groups vary primarily in relative amounts of lead and copper, and De Atley argues that they represent different technological alternatives, or recipes, that potters used to produce glazes with specific physical properties.

There is evidence, however, that at least some Pueblo glazes were not particularly complex. Herhahn (1995) states that early Rio Grande glaze paint technology was flexible in that a wide range of lead compositions theoretically could have produced vitreous paints. Glaze paint replication experiments (Herhahn and Blinman 1999) shed some light on the variables needed to produce a vitreous paint. In these experiments, Herhahn and Blinman were able to achieve paint vitrification on ceramic test tiles using a simple mixture of powdered galena and water. The glaze replication data led Herhahn (2006) to propose that Rio Grande potters applied a mixture of manganese with copper or lead to slipped vessels, then wood-fired them once, probably in shallow pits. She argued that much of the silica and alumina found in Rio Grande glazes was introduced via the interaction of metallic oxides (lead, copper, and manganese) with the slip clay over which the mixture was applied (Herhahn 2006). These findings suggested that Rio Grande glaze technology did not necessarily involve the use of glaze recipes requiring multiple raw materials in specific proportions, although the selection of an effective flux (lead) does appear to have been important.

Because the issue of glaze paint complexity has implications not only for the development of distinct glaze paint recipes, but also for the scale of procurement and trade of lead ores, an outline of what I perceive to be the key variables involved in glaze paint manufacture is useful. There are four things that a potter would need to control to make a glaze: raw material selection and combination, firing temperature, firing atmosphere, and length of firing. The three key raw materials are a metallic flux (most often lead), silica, and alumina. Although the exact amount of lead ore needed probably varies from pot to pot, glaze replication experiments by Herhahn in 2003 showed that a small piece of galena (roughly the diameter of a quarter) would be needed to complete glaze framing lines on a 20–cm diameter Rio Grande Glaze C vessel. I expect that it would take a similar amount to paint a Zuni glaze-decorated bowl. Other ingredients (silica, alumina, and colorants) might have been added in smaller proportions to the glaze mixture (Jones 1995) or introduced into the glaze during the firing process (Herhahn 2006). An additional aspect of raw material selection is whether the ores potters used contained impurities (like copper or manganese) that could affect the color of the resulting glaze. Controlling this variable may have been difficult because it would require that potters know something about the properties of various ore sources.

In terms of firing glaze-decorated bowls, potters would need to have control over the firing temperature, atmosphere, and duration to produce a red or white slip and a glaze paint that is neither overfired (bubbly or too runny) or underfired (not completely vitrified). It is possible that potters could, through experimentation, achieve glaze paints without formal instruction in glaze preparation (Herhahn 2006). Indeed, some of the low lead, incompletely vitrified glazes discussed later in this chapter likely are the result of experimentation. At the very least, however, potters would initially need to be told (or given) the correct materials to use as fluxes (such as lead ore). Thus, some degree of communication among potters would have been necessary to successfully reproduce the basic recipe and proper firing conditions required to create a vitreous paint. Once this basic glaze mixture was achieved, potters could have used variable proportions of fluxes and colorants to produce distinctive glaze recipes.

ELECTRON MICROPROBE METHODOLOGY

I used an electron microprobe to measure glaze paint compositions for 313 St. Johns Polychrome, Heshotauthla Polychrome, and Kwakina Polychrome glazes, which were used in turn to assess whether Zuni region potters developed alternative glaze paint recipes. Potters began experimenting with glaze paints toward the late end of the White Mountain Red Ware tradition, to which the type St. Johns Polychrome is assigned by archaeologists. St. Johns Polychrome vessels exhibit a wide range of paint textures, ranging from dull matte to well-vitrified glazes. My sample includes only St. Johns Polychrome sherds exhibiting some degree of paint vitrification, although many of the paints on these sherds would be classified as "subglazes" rather than fully vitrified glazes. These sherds came from contexts mainly post-dating A.D. 1275 (Chapter 2).

As discussed in detail by Reed (1993), the electron microprobe measures the concentrations of major, minor, and trace elements present in a given sample. This technique is particularly suited to the analysis of glazes because it uses a focused electron beam, allowing the researcher to analyze a small area of a cross-section of a sample (Goffer 1980). The electron microprobe has been used to determine the chemical compositions of paints (Steinberg and Kamilli 1984; Wright 1984), glasses (Brill and Moll 1963; Heck and Hoffmann 2000), ceramic pastes (Abbott 2000; De Atley and others 1982), and glazes (De Atley 1986; Herhahn 1995; Huntley and Herhahn 1996; Jones 1995; Matson 1985; Rye and Evans 1976).

Sample preparation for electron microprobe analysis consists of cutting a cross-section from each sherd with a diamond saw, mounting the cross section on a glass slide, and highly polishing the sample surface. The resulting thick section is made conductive by coating it with a thin layer of carbon.

The microprobe works by directing a focused beam of high-energy electrons at a flat, conductive thick section held under a vacuum. With the built-in optical microscope and backscatter electron imaging, the analyst can observe and select an area of the sample's surface to be analyzed. Heavy elements appear brighter in the backscatter image, facilitating easy identification of areas containing lead glaze. The electron beam excites an area of the sample as small as 1 micron in diameter, from which energy and X-rays in wavelengths characteristic of particular elements are emitted. A wavelength-dispersive (WDS) detector records the intensities, or peaks, of the characteristic wavelengths. Each peak is superimposed on a background of the continuous X-ray spectrum, which must be subtracted from the reading (Reed 1993). Following background corrections, readings from each sample are typically compared with known standards under identical instrument conditions to determine the quantity of a sample's constituent elements (De Atley and others 1982; Freestone 1982; Reed 1993). Details of standard preparation and composition are presented in Huntley (2004, Table 7.1).

Based on my pilot study (Huntley 1997) and previous glaze compositional analyses (Bower and others 1986; De Atley 1986, Huntley and Herhahn 1996), I limited the analysis to twelve major and minor constituents of glazes: aluminum, calcium, copper, iron, lead, magnesium, manganese, potassium, silica, sodium, titanium, and zinc. The microprobe generally offers a level of precision of one to two percent for these elements (Freestone 1982), which falls well within the five percent range considered acceptable for compositional analyses (Bishop and others 1982; Bishop and others 1990). Each element is numerically converted to oxide form by the microprobe software. Typically, five individual readings were taken at different points on each sample thick section, thus averaging out potential heterogeneity inherent in the glaze. Individual point values were then normalized to 100 percent and an average percentage by weight for every oxide was calculated for each glaze sample (Huntley 2004, Table D.1).

GLAZE COMPOSITIONS

Lead or copper (in some cases, both) were major constituents of Zuni region glazes (Table 4.1). The lead used probably was galena (PbS, lead sulfide) or cerrusite ($PbCO_3$, lead carbonate formed via weathering of galena). Unfortunately, sulfur and carbon volatilize during firing and leave few traces in the resulting glaze (carbon could not be measured by the microprobe, even if it were present). Potters probably had several options

Table 4.1. Weight Percentages of Oxides by Ceramic Type

Oxide	St. Johns Polychrome (n = 70)			Heshotauthla Polychrome (n = 153)			Kwakina Polychrome (n = 90)		
	Mean	S.D.	C.V.	Mean	S.D.	C.V.	Mean	S.D.	C.V.
PbO	7.32	12.06	1.647	27.28	15.74	0.577	27.36	17.27	0.631
Cu_2O	17.79	9.66	0.543	13.12	8.65	0.660	11.79	8.10	0.687
SiO_2	43.81	7.98	0.182	37.16	7.96	0.214	37.45	7.86	0.210
Al_2O_3	15.06	4.28	0.284	10.76	4.80	0.446	12.44	6.02	0.484
FeO	4.97	2.83	0.570	4.55	3.76	0.826	3.90	4.12	1.056
K_2O	4.93	2.52	0.511	2.58	2.15	0.833	2.42	2.69	1.110
CaO	2.41	1.15	0.476	1.97	1.24	0.632	2.27	1.93	0.850
MgO	2.19	1.74	0.794	1.21	0.76	0.631	1.08	0.76	0.703
TiO_2	0.64	0.45	0.709	0.43	0.28	0.641	0.51	0.38	0.746
Na_2O	0.39	0.21	0.527	0.25	0.20	0.796	0.19	.13	0.696
MnO	0.36	1.54	4.262	0.54	1.66	3.082	0.45	1.93	4.288
ZnO	0.13	0.41	3.060	0.18	0.46	2.605	0.16	0.46	2.886

for copper, including azurite and malachite (copper carbonates). Other elements present in Zuni glazes probably came either from slip clay intentionally added to the paint mixture or from reactions between the metallic oxides and the underlying slip (Herhahn 2006). The composition of "standard red clay" reported by Denio (1980: 273) can be used for general comparative purposes (57% silica, 19.2% alumina, 6.7% iron, 3.1% magnesium, 4.3% calcium, 2.4% sodium, 2.0% potassium, 0.9% titanium, and 0.9% other oxides). Although the oxide proportions reported in Table 4.1 do not perfectly match these values, they are certainly similar enough to suggest that some type of slip clay was a likely glaze constituent. I also observed several glazes that contained quartz grains within the glass matrix. This quartz may have been introduced intentionally as sand, as Shepard (1942) suggests, or may represent particles naturally occurring in the lead ore matrix.

The microprobe analysis revealed differences in the relative amounts of lead and copper present in Zuni region glaze paints. The greatest difference was that paints on vessels of St. Johns Polychrome, the earliest type on which glazes appeared, tended to have little or no lead and higher amounts of copper compared to paints on vessels of Kwakina Polychrome and Heshotauthla Polychrome (Table 4.1, note shaded values). The average lead composition of sampled St. Johns Polychrome glazes was around seven percent by weight and half of all samples contained less than one percent lead by weight. Copper ranged from less than one percent to

47 percent by weight in St. Johns Polychrome, with a mean of approximately 18 percent. These means can be contrasted with a mean of around 28 percent by weight for lead and around 12 percent by weight for copper in the glazes of later Heshotauthla and Kwakina polychromes. Importantly, lead compositions were not normally distributed (Huntley 2004, Figs. 7.1–7.3). St. Johns Polychrome glazes had a strong peak between 0–5 percent and another smaller peak between 20–25 percent by weight lead oxide. Heshotauthla Polychrome and Kwakina Polychrome glazes exhibited peaks between 0–5 percent and around 35–36 percent by weight lead oxide. I argue later in this chapter that these peaks or modes correspond to separate recipes for glaze paint manufacture (Huntley 2004, 2006). Copper oxide compositions appeared to more closely approximate a normal curve for all three types (Huntley 2004, Figs. 7.4–7.6).

Experimentation with Glaze Paints

The trend toward high lead and low copper appears to have been a gradual development characterized by experimentation with lead-based glaze recipes at the late end of the White Mountain Red Ware sequence and the beginning of the ancestral Zuni glaze-decorated ware sequence. Three lines of evidence point to experimentation with glaze paints by potters attempting to perfect the technique: compositional overlap between late St. Johns Polychrome and early Heshotauthla and Kwakina polychromes, decreased compositional variability in Heshotauthla and Kwakina polychromes, and improved vitrification in high lead glazes, particularly for Heshotauthla and Kwakina polychromes.

Figures 4.1 and 4.2 show box-and-whisker plots of lead and copper percentages by weight for St. Johns Polychrome, Heshotauthla Polychrome, and Kwakina Polychrome from early and late Pueblo IV archaeological contexts (Chapter 2). The box-and-whisker plots present median values rather than means and they highlight the presence of a few outliers for each pottery type. As the two figures indicate, within earlier archaeological contexts, all three types have lower median values for lead than do all three types from later contexts. The fact that St. Johns glaze compositions overlap substantially with early Heshotauthla and Kwakina glaze compositions suggests that the change from low lead/high copper paints to high lead paints did not occur suddenly, but rather involved a period of experimentation with the new high lead recipe.

Further evidence that potters gradually developed a high lead recipe that allowed them to more consistently produce well vitrified paints is provided by the observation that glazes on Kwakina and Heshotauthla polychromes became less compositionally variable through time. Table 4.2 presents coefficients of variation for key glaze components by ceramic type from early and late archaeological contexts. I computed coefficients of variation using molecular proportions for each oxide, which are calculated by dividing an oxide's weight percent by its molecular weight. The molecular proportion therefore represents the proportion of molecules for each oxide present in the mixture and ensures that heavy elements, such as lead, do not have disproportionate influence on statistical analyses.

As the table indicates, both Heshotauthla and Kwakina polychromes from late contexts are less variable than are both types from earlier contexts, a trend that St. Johns Polychrome glazes do not share. St. Johns glazes are consistently more heterogeneous (and lower) in lead compositions compared to Kwakina and Heshotauthla polychromes. Such variability in the major fluxing ingredient would have resulted in inconsistent glaze vitrification. Increased compositional homogeneity in Kwakina and Heshotauthla glazes might be explained by increased standardization in glaze recipes through time, due either to a reduction of the number of glaze producers, decreased variability in raw materials, or the result of a general consensus among Zuni region potters

Table 4.2. Coefficients of Variation for Molecular Proportions of Major Glaze Components by Ceramic Type and Time Period

Ceramic Type	Oxide	Early Contexts	Late Contexts
Heshotauthla Polychrome		n = 50	n = 94
	Lead	0.907	0.433
	Copper	0.714	0.632
	Alumina	0.507	0.402
	Silica	0.237	0.205
Kwakina Polychrome		n = 24	n = 64
	Lead	1.115	0.490
	Copper	0.651	0.661
	Alumina	0.509	0.473
	Silica	0.233	0.189
St. Johns Polychrome		n = 53	n = 15
	Lead	1.601	1.525
	Copper	0.493	0.671
	Alumina	0.268	0.320
	Silica	0.185	0.189

NOTE: Oxide compositions calculated using molecular proportions for each oxide.

about the appropriate way to make a glaze. A more consistent glaze recipe, particularly if coupled with consistent ore sources and improved processing techniques, would have allowed potters to reliably achieve certain glaze qualities, such as glassiness and color brightness. More uniform glaze qualities are exactly what we see in the majority of Heshotauthla Polychrome and Kwakina Polychrome glazes.

The amount of flux present in a particular glaze paint plays a major role in determining the extent of vitrification that can be achieved. Thus, the relatively low lead and high silica and alumina in many St. Johns Polychrome glazes (Table 4.1) may explain why many of them are not uniformly vitreous and are best considered subglazes. The distinction between glaze and subglaze paints, however, is not as simple as overall lead content. Many of the subglaze paints included in this study may actually be on weathered or possibly misfired vessels. Furthermore, Shepard (1942: 220) notes that the higher the percentage of lead in a glaze, the more it is subject to leaching by soil moisture and that lead would be leached out sooner than other elements. Differential

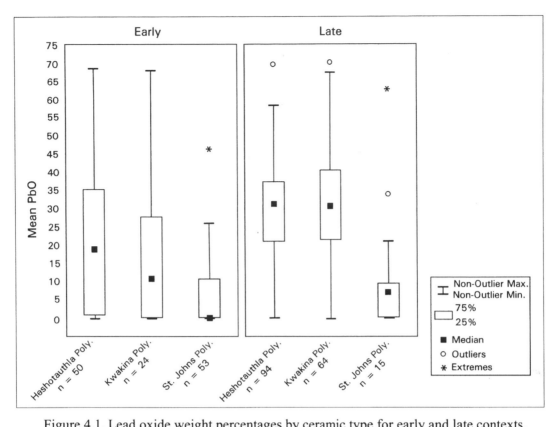

Figure 4.1. Lead oxide weight percentages by ceramic type for early and late contexts.

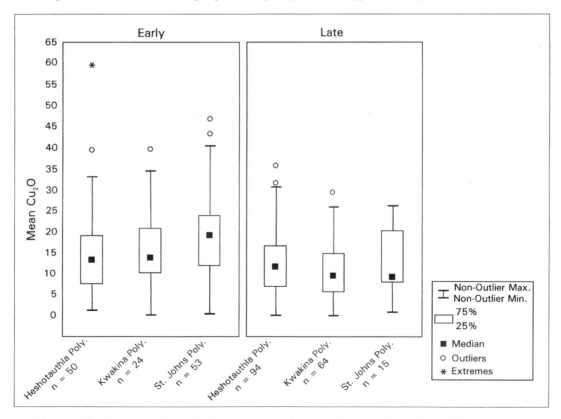

Figure 4.2. Copper oxide weight percentages by ceramic type for early and late contexts.

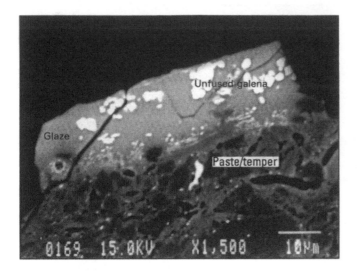

Figure 4.3. A heterogeneous glaze with low lead (9% by weight) and high copper (32% by weight).

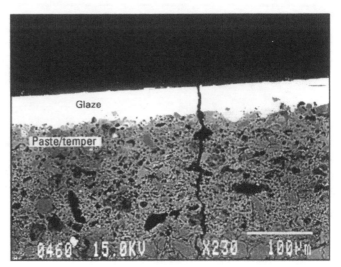

Figure 4.4. A vitreous glaze with high lead (35% by weight) and low copper (6% by weight). Magnification level is less than in Figure 4.3.

weathering of some sherds may therefore cause some high lead paints to appear less shiny. The extent of glaze vitrification is also related to the process of preparing and mixing glaze ingredients; for example, how well a potter was able to grind the raw ore into small, easily melted particles. The firing process almost certainly would have contributed to vitrification as well, and glassier glaze paints were likely fired at higher temperatures or were more completely oxidized than subglaze paints.

Microscopic examination of glazes with low levels of lead revealed that a large number of the sherds contained abundant unfused particles, indicating that incomplete vitrification occurred during firing. Figure 4.3 shows a representative low lead glaze. The unfused, bright Cu and Pb crystals are visible under high magnification within the glaze matrix and indistinct interface between glaze and underlying slip. It can be difficult to avoid these particles with the microprobe (particularly if the entire glaze consists of unfused matter), and chemical compositions for these partially vitrified glazes tend to be variable. I interpret many of these paints lacking an actual glaze layer to be experiments that were often not entirely successful. Herhahn (2006: 193) reports similar characteristics in many early Rio Grande glaze paints, which she also interprets as resulting from experimentation by potters learning glaze production techniques. In contrast, high lead glazes in my sample tended to be glassier and less internally variable, as shown in Figure 4.4; in this example there is a dis-

tinct boundary between the bright, uniform glaze and darker, heterogeneous clay paste.

The data that I interpret as evidence for experimentation with glaze paints by Zuni region potters have two important implications. First, they suggest that fully developed glaze paint technology was not simply passed along from other glaze producing areas, such as the Mogollon Mountains, via migration or other mechanisms. Second, because both high and low lead paints were found at all nucleated pueblos included in my study, it appears that potters within the Zuni region communicated the results of their experiments and shared with their neighbors the information needed to consistently produce vitreous paints.

Glaze Recipes

I performed a k-means nonhierarchical cluster analysis (Kintigh 2002) to identify groups of glaze samples with similar compositions using standardized z-scores of the molecular proportions for each oxide and incorporated all samples independent of type or time period to create compositional groups. A three-cluster solution exhibited the most pronounced difference from randomly generated data and confirmed the major distinction between high and low lead paints (see Huntley 2004, Table D.3 for k-means output). It also identified a third, smaller compositional group characterized by high levels of manganese. Other cluster solutions resulted in further partitioning of the two large

Table 4.3. Summary Statistics for Oxide Molecular Proportions by K-Means Group

Oxide	Group 1 (n = 155)			Group 2 (n = 18)			Group 3 (n = 140)		
	Mean	S.D.	C.V.	Mean	S.D.	C.V.	Mean	S.D.	C.V.
PbO	0.163	0.052	0.318	0.115	0.063	0.551	0.033	0.038	1.148
Cu_2O	0.085	0.057	0.671	0.079	0.074	0.936	0.111	0.065	0.583
SiO_2	0.563	0.100	0.178	0.611	0.136	0.223	0.739	0.116	0.157
Al_2O_3	0.088	0.031	0.351	0.097	0.036	0.368	0.157	0.048	0.307
FeO	0.051	0.043	0.846	0.053	0.039	0.741	0.075	0.058	0.770
K_2O	0.016	0.013	0.826	0.020	0.012	0.625	0.053	0.027	0.519
CaO	0.032	0.025	0.798	0.038	0.027	0.725	0.046	0.025	0.545
MgO	0.023	0.017	0.758	0.027	0.015	0.584	0.048	0.033	0.678
TiO_2	0.004	0.003	0.630	0.006	0.003	0.544	0.008	0.005	0.630
Na_2O	0.002	0.001	0.617	0.005	0.003	0.536	0.006	0.003	0.545
MnO	0.002	0.007	3.360	0.083	0.058	0.700	0.002	0.008	3.751
ZnO	0.001	0.003	2.069	0.013	0.016	1.255	0.001	0.003	2.483

Table 4.4. Results of Between-Group T-Tests

Oxide	Group 1 vs. Group 3			Group 1 vs. Group 2			Group 3 vs. Group 2		
	T value	D.F.	Prob.	T value	D.F.	Prob.	T value	D.F.	Prob.
PbO	24.190	293	0.0000	3.661	171	0.0003	7.7544	156	0.0000
Cu_2O	-3.680	293	0.0003	0.421	171	0.6741	-1.9589	156	0.0519
SiO_2	-14.014	293	0.0000	-1.848	171	0.0663	-4.3319	156	0.0001
Al_2O_3	-14.739	293	0.0000	-1.140	171	0.2560	-5.0921	156	0.0000
FeO	-4.053	293	0.0001	-0.126	171	0.8998	-1.6105	156	0.1093
K_2O	-15.134	293	0.0000	-1.329	171	0.1856	-5.0200	156	0.0000
CaO	-4.636	293	0.0000	-0.915	171	0.3615	-1.2331	156	0.2194
MgO	-8.531	293	0.0000	-0.885	171	0.3775	-2.7897	156	0.0059
TiO_2	0.480	293	0.6319	0.284	171	0.7769	-2.0812	156	0.0391
Na_2O	0.602	293	0.5478	0.258	171	0.7967	-1.5873	156	0.1145
MnO	0.018	293	0.9857	-16.692	171	0.0000	15.7582	156	0.0000
ZnO	0.983	293	0.3265	-0.154	171	0.8776	7.8259	156	0.0000

NOTE: Shaded values are significant at 0.05 probability level.

compositional groups, but these solutions largely highlighted differences in minor elements, such as magnesium, titanium, and zinc, that were highly variable and present in prehistoric glazes as impurities associated with other minerals. I chose to focus on the three-cluster solution because I believe it distinguishes groups that are the result of intentional glaze preparation strategies used by Zuni region potters and because it is congruent with the lead compositional modes identified earlier in this chapter.

Descriptive statistics for each group are presented in Table 4.3. As the results of t-tests presented in Table 4.4 indicate, Groups 1 and 3 differ significantly in lead, copper, iron, alumina, silica, magnesium, calcium, and potassium concentrations. A total of 60 percent of all sampled Heshotauthla Polychrome glazes and 61 percent of Kwakina Polychrome glazes are classified in Group 1 (Table 4.5). Only 11 percent of St. Johns Polychrome glazes are classified in this group. Group 3, the low lead group, contains 84 percent of all St. Johns Polychrome glazes and 33 percent and 34 percent, respectively, of Heshotauthla and Kwakina glazes. Group 2 appears to be a lower lead/higher manganese version of Group 1 (Table 4.5). There are a number of significant differences between Group 2 and Group 3, the most important of which probably are in lead, copper, manganese, silica, and alumina concentrations (Table 4.4). Group 2 contains relatively low frequencies

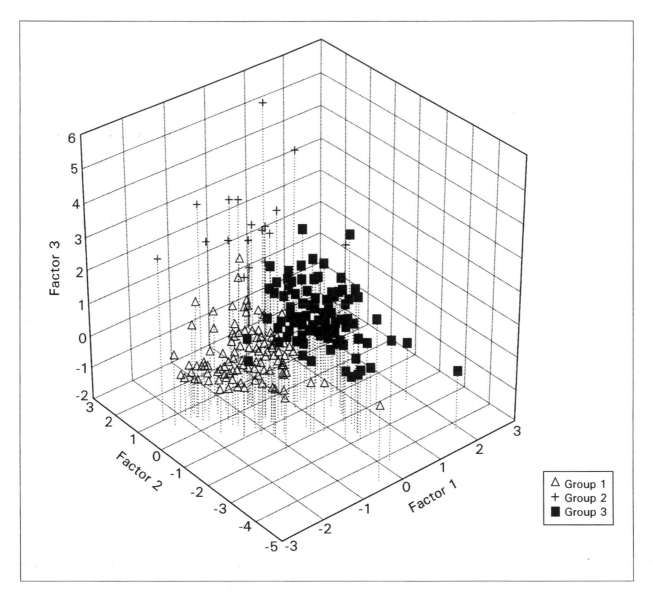

Figure 4.5. Plot of factor scores by K-means compositional group.

of all three types, although Heshotauthla Polychrome glazes are most common (Table 4.5).

A Principal Components Analysis (PCA) using oxide molecular proportions confirms the patterns observed above. Figure 4.5, a plot of sample factor scores for components 1–3, graphically illustrates cluster separation. Together these components account for 55 percent of all variability present in the dataset. For component 1, lead shows a strong negative loading and silica, alumina, sodium, and potassium have strong positive loadings; copper loads heavily on component 2 and manganese loads heavily on component 3 (see Huntley 2004, Table D.4 for supporting statistics).

Table 4.5. Ceramic Types by Glaze Compositional Group

| | Glaze Comp. Group (Row %) | | |
| | 1 | 2 | 3 |
Ceramic type	(high Pb)	(high Mn)	(low Pb)
Heshotauthla Poly.			
(n = 153)	60.1%	7.2%	32.7%
Kwakina Poly.			
(n = 90)	61.1%	4.4%	34.4%
St. Johns Poly.			
(n = 70)	11.4%	4.3%	84.3%
Total (n = 313)	*49.5%*	*5.8%*	*44.7%*

**Table 4.6. Glaze Compositional Groups by
Production Source and Time Period**

Production Source	Glaze Comp. Group (Row %)		
	1 (high Pb) n = 52	2 (high Mn) n = 7	3 (low Pb) n = 59
Early Contexts			
El Morro (n = 6)	-	-	100.0%
Pescado (n = 25)	44.0%	8.0%	48.0%
North (n = 12)	8.3%	8.3%	83.4%
Southwest (n = 7)	-	-	100.0%
Early Total (n = 50)	24.0%	6.0%	70.0%
Late Contexts			
El Morro (n = 14)	35.7%	7.1%	57.2%
Pescado (n = 49)	67.4%	6.1%	26.5%
Southwest (n = 5)	40.0%	-	60.0%
Late Total (n = 68)	58.8%	5.9%	35.3%

These three compositional groups involve simple yet critical differences in the way glazes are formulated and I conclude that they represent different recipes developed by Zuni region potters. An examination of intraregional patterning in glaze recipes reveals that although the basic glaze recipe seems to have changed through time at all of the sampled pueblos within the Zuni region, there are some subtle differences among pueblos in how quickly the high lead recipe was adopted. Glaze compositional data for 118 samples can be attributed to a particular production source based on INAA and assigned to either early or late Pueblo IV contexts (Chapters 2 and 3). For this comparison I assume that batches, or prepared mixtures, of glaze paints were not traded independently of ceramic vessels, as has been suggested by Habicht-Mauche and others (2000), a point I return to in Chapter 5. As Table 4.6 indicates, low lead paints (Group 3) are generally more common overall than high lead paints (Group 1) on vessels recovered from early contexts. However, in early contexts, high lead glazes are common on vessels argued to have been made at Heshotauthla Pueblo in the Pescado Basin but absent on vessels from the El Morro Valley. The likelihood of obtaining a pattern this strong or stronger at random is low (Fisher's Exact test p = 0.06). All seven of the early context glaze paints from the southwestern portion of the Zuni region are low lead glazes. Fisher's Exact test produces a probability of .03 that the distribution of low lead paints would be this different or more

different between the Pescado Basin and Southwest production zones. In later contexts, high lead paints are on average about twice as common on vessels produced in the Pescado Basin as on vessels attributed to the El Morro Valley or Jaralosa Draw (Southwest cluster). Again, a distribution this extreme or more extreme is unlikely to have occurred at random (Fisher's Exact p = 0.05). The small number of high manganese paints do not show any strong patterning by production source, although no high manganese paints are attributed to the Southwest production zone.

I cannot completely rule out the possibility that differences in high lead glaze recipes between the El Morro Valley pueblos and other parts of the Zuni region are, at least in part, an effect of time. One explanation for the scarcity of high lead paints from the El Morro Valley and northern Zuni region is that the Box S and Mirabal assemblages came from early contexts and predate the development of high lead paint recipes. However, assemblages from several proveniences at other sites appear to be even earlier than these two assemblages. Thus, although there was a strong temporal component to the use of lead versus copper-based glaze recipes within the Zuni region as a whole, potters from pueblos in different parts of the region appear to have adopted the high lead recipe at different times.

Glaze Colors

Using a paint mixture relatively high in lead would have been advantageous not only because a high lead glaze is more likely to vitrify, but also because a lead-silica glaze is essentially clear, so that its color can be easily manipulated using small amounts of iron, manganese, or copper. However, glaze color is a complex property that depends not only on the types and quantities of colorants added, but also on their oxidation state, firing temperature and conditions (for example, reducing or oxidizing atmosphere), and thickness of the glaze (Hawley 1938). Moreover, interactions among different colorants (primarily iron, copper, and manganese) present in many of the Zuni glazes may have made it difficult for potters working with this new technology to consistently produce particular colors. Iron oxide, for example, can be used to produce a variety of colors ranging from light green or yellow to reddish brown or black depending on firing conditions and presence or absence of other minerals (Green 1973; Rhodes 1973). Underlying slip color also has an effect on observed

Table 4.7. Distribution of Glaze Colors Among Compositional Groups by Percent

| | Glaze Compositional Group (Column %) | | | |
| | 1 (high Pb) | 2 (high Mn) | 3 (low Pb) | Total |
Glaze Color (n:	155	18	140	313)
Black (n = 170)	47.1	44.4	63.5	54.3
Brown (n = 6)	0.7	5.6	2.9	1.9
Green (n = 118)	45.7	44.4	27.9	37.7
Purple (n = 11)	2.6	5.6	4.3	3.5
Red (n = 8)	3.9	-	1.4	2.6

Table 4.8. Classification Success Percentages by Glaze Color for Compositional Groups

| Glaze Color | Compositional Group | | |
	1	2	3
Black	41	63	52
Green	69	50	5
Purple	50	-	17
Red	50	-	-
Brown	-	-	75
Total	*53*	*56*	*37*

glaze color. A green glaze on a white-slipped Kwakina Polychrome bowl, for example, appears brighter than it would on a red-slipped St. Johns or Heshotauthla Polychrome bowl.

To determine whether particular pueblos or pueblo clusters consistently used particular glaze colors, I recorded interior glaze color for all decorated sherds selected for electron microprobe analysis. The Munsell soil color chart could not be used to record glaze color because it does not include appropriate reference standards for vitreous material. My approach to the classification of glaze color in this study was to create broad color categories (for example, black, green, brown). I then assigned individual samples to a particular color category based on comparison with other samples in that category. The recorded glaze colors are subjective, but since I coded all of the colors myself, the observations are at least internally consistent. I recorded both interior and exterior glaze colors; however, because the occurrence of glaze paint on bowl exteriors is rare (n = 63), only interior glaze colors are discussed here.

Table 4.7 shows the distribution of glaze colors among the three glaze compositional groups identified earlier in this chapter. Although the pattern is not particularly strong, brightly colored green glazes are more common in the high lead and high manganese groups (1 and 2) than in the low lead group (Group 3). Black paints, on the other hand, are more common in Group 3. Fisher's Exact test indicates that proportions of black versus green paints as different as those observed in Groups 1 and 3 are unlikely to occur at random (two-tailed p = 0.002).

I performed a discriminant analysis (Baxter 1994: 186) to evaluate how well certain glaze constituents predict glaze color for each compositional group. I used the stepwise discriminant analysis procedure available in STATISTICA for Windows to evaluate classification success rates by glaze compositional group using combinations of glaze colorants (iron oxide, copper oxide, and manganese oxide) with lead. One advantage of the stepwise method is that it constructs a step-by-step model of discrimination, in which variables that do not contribute to prediction of group membership at a selected level of statistical significance are excluded. Color categories represented by a single case for a particular group had to be excluded from the analysis. As shown in Table 4.8, for Group 3 (low lead), discriminant analysis correctly classifies only 37 percent of all cases by color. Lead and copper are the variables used to predict group membership and iron and manganese were removed from the model, indicating that they are not reliable predictors of glaze color. For Group 1 (high lead), copper, iron, and manganese are all important in distinguishing color but lead is not. This group has a better classification success rate by color of 53 percent. Green glazes, in particular, are classified correctly nearly 70 percent of the time based on relative proportions of colorants. For Group 2 (high manganese) the classification success rate is 56 percent using all three colorants and lead. My interpretation of these results is that with higher lead compositions, as in Group 1, color can be more consistently predicted based on the proportions of colorant oxides. Lead essentially has no effect on color. In the low lead group (Group 3), the strong coloring effects of copper are probably swamping the effects of other colorants, which may also be the case for Group 2.

Examination of the 124 sherds from early or late contexts (Chapter 2) that could be assigned to a particular production source based on paste composition (Chapter 3) revealed an overall increase through time in

Table 4.9. Percentages of Glaze Colors by Production Source

Production Source	(n:	Black 72	Brown 5	Green 38	Purple 6	Red 3)
			Early Contexts			
El Morro (n = 6)		83.3	-	16.7	-	-
Pescado (n = 26)		69.2	11.5	15.4	-	3.9
North (n = 15)		53.3	13.3	26.7	6.7	-
Southwest (n = 7)		100	-	-	-	-
Total (n = 54)		*70.3*	*9.3*	*16.6*	*1.9*	*1.9*
			Late Contexts			
El Morro (n = 13)		69.2	-	23.1	7.7	-
Pescado (n = 50)		40.0	-	48.0	8.0	4.0
Southwest (n = 6)		66.7	-	33.3	-	-
Total (n = 69)		*47.8*	-	*42.0*	*7.3*	*2.9*

Table 4.10. Descriptions of Slip Color Groups

Group	Munsell Hues	Descriptions
Red-Slipped Ware (Heshotauthla and St. Johns Polychrome)		
1 (Red)	10R	light red to red
2 (Orange)	2.5YR	light reddish brown to red
	5YR	reddish brown to reddish yellow
	7.5YR	brown to reddish yellow
3 (Yellow)	10YR	grayish brown to brownish yellow
	2.5Y	light yellowish brown to yellow
	5Y	olive gray
White-Slipped Ware (Kwakina Polychrome)		
1 (Pink-White)	2.5YR	pinkish white
	5YR	pink to gray
	7.5YR	pinkish gray to pink
2 (Cream)	10YR	light gray to very pale brown
	2.5Y	white to pale yellow
	5Y	light gray to white

the proportions of green glazes at all production source areas (Table 4.9). Notably, there were no strong associations among particular glaze colors and production sources. In my sample, black glazes appeared to be slightly more common in the El Morro Valley for both early and late contexts and green glazes appeared to be slightly more common in the Pescado Basin (late contexts) or North (early contexts) production zones. However, Fisher's Exact tests performed on three aggregated glaze color categories (black, green, and all other colors combined) for pairs of production sources produced probabilities of .5 or greater, indicating that glaze color distributions as different or more different than the observed distributions have at least a 50 percent probability of occurring at random. Based on these results, I concluded that potters from different parts of the Zuni region did not consistently use particular glaze colors on their ceramic vessels and that glaze color is not a good indicator of interactions at the pueblo or pueblo cluster level.

SLIP COLORS

Previous studies of slip colors on ancestral Zuni glaze-decorated vessels and White Mountain Red Ware document temporal variability in slip color within the Zuni region. LeBlanc's (1975, 1976) attribute analysis of St. Johns Polychrome and Heshotauthla Polychrome sherds from late Pueblo III and Pueblo IV contexts in the El Morro Valley and pueblos located along the

Nutria River (just north of Heshotauthla Pueblo) indicates that red slips (Munsell hue 10R) were more common in earlier contexts, whereas orange slips (Munsell hues 2.5YR, 5YR) were common later. Kintigh's (1985b) detailed attribute analysis of ceramic assemblages from the El Morro Valley produces similar results in that orange colors (Munsell hues 2.5YR, 5YR) are typically associated with vitreous paints, which tend to be more common in later contexts (see Chapter 2).

In this study, I recorded exterior and interior slip colors using the Munsell color chart for all decorated sherds selected for electron microprobe analysis (n = 333). I did not record slip color on extremely burned or weathered sherds. Munsell slip colors were then classified into hue groups (three groups for red slips; two for white slips; Table 4.10). These groups were intentionally broad because slips often were variable on the same vessel due to color transfer between glaze and slip and to weathering or fire clouding. My red slip groups generally corresponded with those used by LeBlanc (1975, 1976) and Kintigh (1985b), although I recorded a small number of brownish yellow slips (Group 3) that they did not. For red slips, colors in Group 1 tended to be darker red; colors in Group 2 were more orange, and colors in Group 3, which was relatively uncommon, were more yellow. For white slips, colors in Group 1 were generally pinkish white, whereas colors in Group 2 had more of a yellowish tint and were more cream-colored.

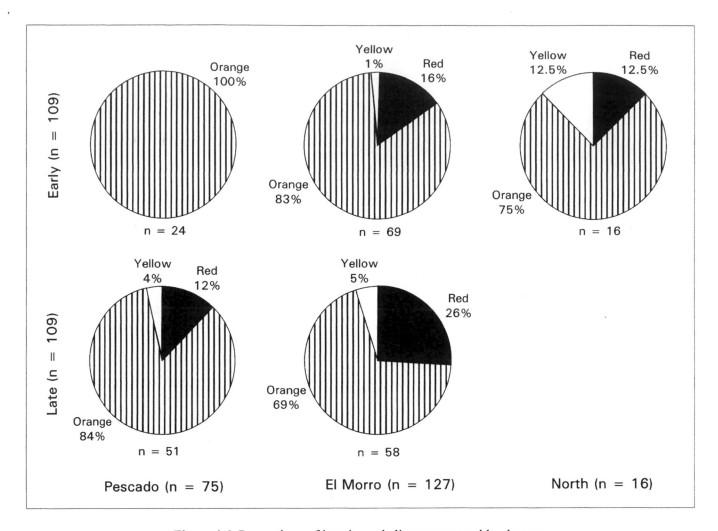

Figure 4.6. Proportions of interior red slips among pueblo clusters.

Analysis of Munsell color data for interior and exterior slip colors on St. Johns Polychrome, Heshotauthla Polychrome, and Kwakina Polychrome revealed region-wide similarities in the proportions of both interior and exterior red slips on Heshotauthla and St. Johns. In contrast, cream-colored slips on Kwakina Polychrome became more common than pinkish white slips through time, but were especially common in the El Morro Valley.

Pie charts showing the proportions of red, orange, and yellow interior and exterior slips on St. Johns Polychrome and Heshotauthla Polychrome sampled from early and late contexts are in Figures 4.6 and 4.7. In both figures, slip colors are aggregated by pueblo cluster. Both figures show a preponderance of orange slips across the Zuni region. For all three ceramic types, orange exterior slip colors are consistently more com-

mon than red or yellow slips. The persistence of a small number of red slips, however, is intriguing. Both Le-Blanc (1975, 1976) and Kintigh (1985b) observed a shift from red slips to orange slips on vessels from contexts that predate those analyzed here. Although I would expect my sample to reflect this general trend, the proportions of red slips, in fact, unexpectedly increases in the mid–A.D.1300s. This increase is most evident on pottery from the El Morro Valley, where red slips comprised 26 percent of all interior slips and 19 percent of all exterior slips from late contexts.

I show proportions of red, yellow, and orange slips both for vessel interiors and exteriors because there is not always direct correspondence between interior and exterior color. Compare, for example, the proportions of these three colors for interior versus exterior slips from Pescado Basin pueblos (Figs. 4.6 and 4.7). Differences

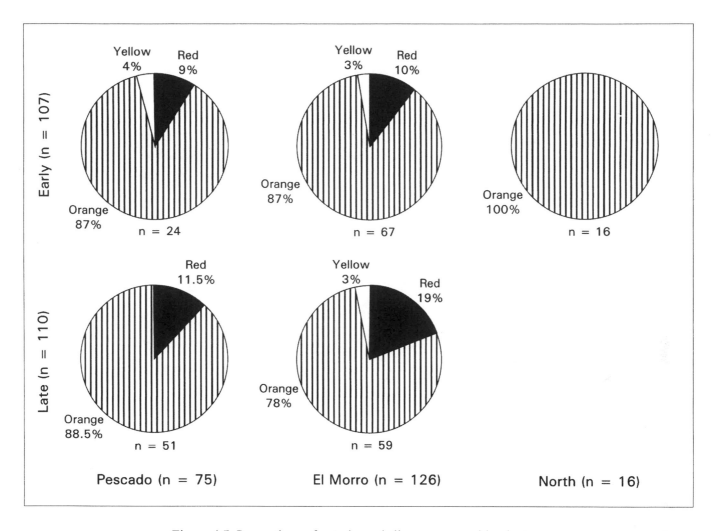

Figure 4.7. Proportions of exterior red slips among pueblo clusters.

in interior versus exterior color might be attributed in part to firing conditions (for example, variable oxidation or fire clouding) or inconsistent recording of Munsell color, but a pilot study of slip compositions using Laser Ablation Inductively-Coupled Plasma Mass Spectrometry (LA-ICP-MS) provides evidence that potters occasionally used compositionally distinct slip clays on different sides of a vessel. LA-ICP-MS (Speakman and Neff 2002) is similar to the ICP-MS technique used to determine lead isotope ratios (Chapter 5). One of the main differences between the two techniques, as used here, has to do with sample preparation. LA-ICP-MS differs from traditional ICP-MS in that a laser ablates or vaporizes a small portion of each sample, thus negating the need for prior acid dissolution of sample material.

Due to the small sample size and unsystematic way in which the sample was selected, the results of this

analysis are considered preliminary and are not discussed in detail here, but slip compositions for a small sample of sherds (n = 81) were measured at MURR. For two of these sherds, interior and exterior red slips were compositionally distinct and classified in separate compositional groups (Neff 2002b). In the case of these two sherds, minor differences in iron content between interior and exterior probably explain their slightly different interior and exterior slip colors.

For white slips on Kwakina Polychrome (Fig. 4.8), there was an increase through time from pinkish white to cream slips. Fisher's Exact test on the frequencies of pinkish white versus cream slips from early versus late contexts produces a probability of 0.001, indicating that differences in slip color distribution as great or greater than the observed differences are unlikely to have occurred by chance. Thus, I argue that increased use of

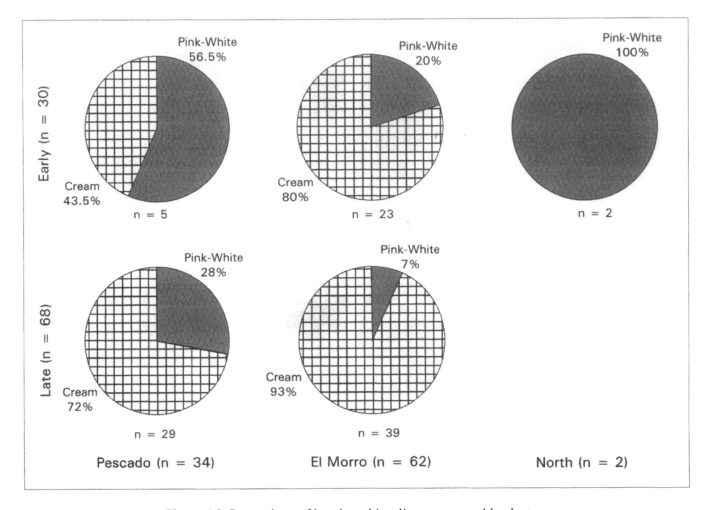

Figure 4.8. Proportions of interior white slips among pueblo clusters.

cream-colored slips through time on Kwakina Polychrome reflects decorative choices made by potters. Not all potters, however, used cream slips. Cream-colored slips appear to have been more common in the El Morro Valley compared to the Pescado Basin, particularly on sampled sherds from late Pueblo IV contexts (Fisher's Exact p = 0.03).

In summary, relative uniformity in the use of slips with particular hues on red-slipped pottery appears to have been normal for the Zuni region, particularly after about A.D. 1325. It is possible that this uniformity was due to resource sharing if red-firing slip clays have restricted geological distributions. White slip color hues were somewhat different between the El Morro Valley and the Pescado Basin, a pattern that would be expected if white slip clays were differentially distributed in these two areas. This pattern would not, however, explain the region-wide increase in cream-colored slips on Kwakina

Polychrome vessels from all production sources through time. Use of particular slip colors may have been related to the use-contexts for glaze-decorated bowls. Slip color was probably the most visible aspect of pottery decoration, and potters who made glaze-decorated vessels used in ritual contexts (such as community feasts) likely conformed to particular conventions in their use of color. Since Heshotauthla Polychrome and St. Johns Polychrome exhibited uniformity in slip color and were also circulated in moderate amounts throughout the Zuni region, I propose that these two types were more commonly used in multipueblo integrative rituals than Kwakina Polychrome. Kwakina pottery is characterized by greater intraregional variability in white slip color, more limited circulation throughout the region, and possibly differential distribution among particular nucleated pueblos (Chapter 2). Kwakina Polychrome may have been intended primarily for local consumption and use, either at the level of the individual household or pueblo.

INTERPRETATIONS

This analysis reveals an overall change through time in Zuni region glaze paint compositions from relatively low lead to relatively high lead and a reduction in compositional variability in later glazes. I interpret variability in early glazes to be the result of experimentation with unfamiliar materials. Comparison of glaze paint compositions with lead isotope data (Chapter 5) suggests that the shift to high lead glazes was not simply a matter of switching raw material sources. Instead, I conclude that compositional modes represent different glaze paint recipes available to Zuni region potters. Lead-based and copper-based recipes represent different technological alternatives that would produce broadly similar products, although high lead composition would have theoretically produced a more uniformly vitreous paint.

Contrary to my expectations and the results of previous glaze paint compositional studies, the data provide no indications that distinctive glaze paint recipes developed among potters residing at particular pueblos. Instead, a high lead recipe appears to have been preferred, eventually, by nearly everyone. A shared basic glaze recipe and increasing homogeneity in glaze compositions through time were the result of intra-regional interactions that facilitated communication among potters. Within the region, however, potters from pueblos in the Pescado Basin appear to have adopted a high lead glaze recipe more completely and earlier than potters in the El Morro Valley or the Jaralosa Draw area. I interpret this discrepancy as indicating that interactions among potters were most intense within pueblo clusters.

Use of high lead glazes should have facilitated more predictable manipulation of glaze colors. Although there seems to have been an increase in the use of brightly colored green glazes through time, possibly facilitated by the use of a higher lead recipe, there is no strong patterning in the use of certain glaze colors by particular

nucleated pueblos. Choice of glaze color, therefore, appears to have been a matter of personal preference for Zuni region potters.

No doubt some of the variability in glaze colors on ancestral Zuni glaze-decorated vessels is due to the inexact nature of Pueblo glaze technology. Potters would surely have known the appropriate proportions of materials to mix together, and they must have had a general sense of the firing temperature and atmosphere needed to produce a glassy paint. However, the recipes that potters used were probably inexact, and impurities introduced into a glaze mixture, whether from the original ore source, from added materials, or from processing techniques like grinding glaze ingredients on sandstone metates that contained copper impurities (Shepard 1942: 221), probably often had unexpected effects on glaze color.

Although I do think that potters attempted to produce certain colors and did so with some success, particularly using a high lead glaze recipe, the specific color of a glaze may not have mattered as much as the finish; that is, that the paint was shiny and highly visible. For Kwakina Polychrome in particular, I propose that the combination of a shiny, high lead glaze and light slip worked together to produce colors that appeared more brilliant to the observer.

The highly visible background slip colors used on polychrome pottery in the Zuni region are fairly uniform, particularly for overall red-slipped Heshotauthla and St. Johns polychromes. Considering their proposed role in integrative ritual contexts during the Pueblo IV period, certain types of glaze-decorated bowls may not have been appropriate media for highlighting social group affiliation thorough stylistic expression. Intra-regional differences in the use of white slip colors on Kwakina Polychrome, however, might indicate that these vessels were used to express different kinds of information in different social contexts. That Kwakina Polychrome was infrequently exchanged within the Zuni region compared to Heshotauthla and St. Johns vessels (Chapter 3) provides some support for an interpretation of this type as primarily for household or individual use.

CHAPTER FIVE

Lead Ore Use and Long-Distance Interaction

Stable lead isotope analysis indicates that potters in the Zuni region utilized multiple ore sources to make glaze paints, although they initially focused on the Cerrillos Hills deposits near present day Santa Fe, New Mexico. A region-wide increase through time in the use of ores from the Magdalena Mountains near Socorro, New Mexico points to possible changes in the scale and direction of interregional social interactions during the A.D. 1300s. Access to long-distance resources and the relationships that they entailed does not appear to have been restricted to certain pueblos or pueblo clusters. However, slightly higher proportions of ores from the Magdalena area in the El Morro Valley ceramic sample suggest that El Morro Valley residents participated in slightly different long-distance social networks than did residents of other parts of the Zuni region.

PRINCIPLES OF LEAD ISOTOPE ANALYSIS

Lead isotope analysis is based on the principle that lead ores from different geological sources and the glaze paints made from them can be distinguished by "fingerprints" of the ratios of the four stable isotopes ^{204}Pb, ^{206}Pb, ^{207}Pb, and ^{208}Pb. Measurable differences in these ratios occur naturally because the relative abundances of lead isotopes change with the radioactive decay of progenitor isotopes ^{238}U, ^{235}U, and ^{232}Th that form ^{206}Pb, ^{207}Pb, and ^{208}Pb respectively (Gulson 1986). There is no additional creation of ^{204}Pb in geologic formations because it has no long-lived radioactive parent. Thus, ratios of lead isotopes in ore deposits vary with their geologic age, parent-daughter isotope ratios, and weathering.

Fractionation is the partial separation of isotopes with different atomic masses as the result of chemical or physical processes. Because there is no isotopic frac-tionation as a result of weathering or cultural practices such as firing (Gulson 1986; Stos-Gale 1992), isotopic conservation enables tracing the origins of lead in glazes to lead ore deposits using comparisons of their isotopic composition.

Lead isotope analysis has proven useful for sourcing a number of archaeological materials, including metallic leads, silver, copper, bronze, faience, glass, glazes, and other pigments (Al-Saa'd 2000; Boni and others 2000; Brill and Wampler 1967; Brill and others 1979; Gale and Stos-Gale 1982; Habicht-Mauche and others 2000; Habicht-Mauche and others 2002; Huntley and others 2007; Stos-Gale 1992; Wolf and others 2003). Habicht-Mauche and her colleagues (2000; and with others 2002) successfully used Hr ICP-MS to match lead ores from mines in the Cerrillos Hills with lead-based glaze paints from Middle Rio Grande Valley archaeological sites. Huntley and others (2007) recently sourced sixteenth- and seventeenth-century glazes from the Salinas pueblos southeast of Albuquerque to the Cerrillos Hills and Magdalena area deposits.

GEOLOGIC DISTRIBUTION AND PREHISTORIC USE OF ORE DEPOSITS

Lead and copper ores occur in association in a number of geological formations throughout New Mexico and Arizona. For the most part, the mineralogy of these ore deposits is well documented, and in some cases there is evidence (documentary or archaeological) that Pueblo populations used them. The following discussion focuses on some of the major New Mexico deposits believed to be important to this study. There are several other deposits that are not covered here, and the reader is referred to File (1965), Northrop (1996), and the U.S. Geological Survey (1969, 1982) for overviews.

The Cerrillos Hills near Santa Fe are famous for their turquoise mines (Warren and Mathien 1985). This area also contains major deposits of lead and copper that have been mined for hundreds of years (Akright 1979; Bice and others 2003; Disbrow and Stoll 1957; Schroeder 1979; Warren and Mathien 1985; Warren and Weber 1979). Evidence of prehistoric mining activity includes tunnels, waste dumps, stone tools, and glaze-decorated ceramics dating at least as early as A.D. 1325 (Bice and others 2003: 10.1–10.3; Warren and Weber 1979: 7). Habicht-Mauche and others (2000; and with others 2002) have shown that potters in the Galisteo Basin used galena exclusively from the Cerrillos Hills source to make glaze paints on Rio Grande Glaze Ware during the Intermediate Glaze Period (A.D. 1425–1515).

The Cerrillos deposits were formed in two distinct but spatially overlapping episodes (the northern and southern stocks) during the late Oligocene and Miocene time periods. Lead occurs in sulfide veins with abundant quartz, some copper sulfides, and manganese, and oxidation has also produced zones of cerrusite (lead carbonate; Disbrow and Stoll 1957: 49–50). Some later lead-zinc veins crosscut copper deposits (Giles 1991: 64).

Other ore sources are located along the Rio Grande rift. The Placitas mining district, located at the northern end of the Sandia Mountains, also has evidence of prehistoric mining of malachite and azurite (copper carbonate minerals). Rio Grande Glaze Ware dating from the early to mid-1500s was found along with stone tools and evidence of quarrying at the Chuchilla de San Francisco mines (Warren and Weber 1979: 10). Mineral deposits in the Placitas district formed during the Sandia uplift from mineralizing fluid derived from Proterozoic granitic pluton emplacement (Brookins and Majumdar 1982). The Tijeras Canyon mining district, encompassing portions of the southern Sandia and northern Manzano Mountains, also contains numerous lead ores, primarily galena, and some copper minerals. The galena-bearing veins are probably Tertiary in age (Elston 1961: 157).

Three significant mining districts, Magdalena, Magdalena North, and Hansonburg, are located near Socorro, New Mexico. The Magdalena mining district, in the Magdalena Mountains west of Socorro, contains abundant galena veins of mid-Tertiary origin (Ewing 1979: 679). Ores in this district were formed by metasomatic replacement of the limestone beds in which they occur (Lindgren and others 1910). The Magdalena North mining district is adjacent to the Magdalena district and it apparently contains distinctive lead deposits (Homer Milford, personal communication 2002).

Unlike the Cerrillos Hills, there is little archaeological or documentary evidence that Pueblo people used ore deposits in the Magdalena area. According to a source from the Chamuscado-Rodriguez expedition (Hammond and Rey 1966), a party traveling south from Puaray in 1582 encountered six mineral deposits about "20 leagues" from the pueblo. These deposits contained supporting walls constructed within the veins and travelers reported that the deposits were "excellent." Hammond and Rey (1966: 110) suggest that the document refers to the Magdalena Mountains, but the distance may be too far. According to Robert Eveleth (Senior Mining Engineer at the New Mexico Bureau of Geology & Mineral Resources) in 2002, although some lead ores might appear on the surface in the Magdalena mining district, the majority of deposits are deeply buried and there is no evidence for prehispanic excavation of these deposits. Nevertheless, some fifteenth- and sixteenth-century lead glazes from the Salinas pueblos apparently were made using Magdalena ores (Huntley and others 2007). Moreover, numerous large late prehistoric and historic period pueblos are located in the vicinity of the Magdalena and Magdalena North mining districts (Marshall and Walt 1984). Several of these pueblos, including Pinnacle Ruin (recently investigated by Lekson and others 2002), contain St. Johns Polychrome and Zuni glaze-decorated pottery, suggesting that Zuni region potters had contact with this area and likely knew about the nearby ore deposits.

The Sierra Oscura Range (Hansonburg District) southeast of Socorro contains isotopically distinctive galena-bearing veins in late Tertiary faults produced by fracture and dislocation following a period of uplift associated with the Rio Grande rift system (Slawson and Austin 1960: 680; Western Mineral Products Company, undated report of about 1918). The Hansonburg district was historically prospected for copper minerals, which occur as both oxides and carbonates. Stone hammers found in caves and bedding plane deposits around the turn of the century attest to prehistoric or early historic utilization of this area (Eveleth 2002; Western Mineral Products Company undated report). The Isleta apparently knew about the Oscura deposits and may have even controlled access to them. Miners establishing claims in the Hansonburg district in the late 1800s were directed to ore sources by Isleta informants, and the miners apparently even purchased some claims from them (Eveleth 2002).

Copper ores are available in the Zuni Mountains (Ferguson and Hart 1985: 49; Lindgren and others 1910) and in parts of south-central Arizona (U.S. Geological Survey 1969). Copper ores in the Zuni Mountains occur in pre-Cambrian rocks and younger Triassic or Permian sedimentary deposits, or "red beds" (Bieberman 1951; Lindgren and others 1910; Maxwell and Nonini 1977). These ores, consisting mainly of the copper carbonates malachite and azurite and, less commonly, chalcopyrite and native copper, outcrop on the surface in several locations (Bieberman 1951; Lindgren and others 1910: 138).

Frank Cushing, who argued that copper was processed and worked in the Southwest prior to European contact, described visiting copper mines with evidence of prehistoric workings in the Zuni Mountains with his Zuni informants (Cushing 1894). He probably collected copper-bearing ores from the vicinity of the present site of Copperton or Sawyer (Hart 1995). A member of Edward Beale's 1959 road-building party reported seeing copper deposits in the Zuni Mountains and in the Ramah Valley (Hart 1984: 35). There are no known reports of lead ores in the Zuni region, however, and no lead ore samples from this area could be located in the geological and archaeological collections that I surveyed.

There is also evidence that the Zuni obtained mineral resources via trade or direct procurement from many parts of the Southwest, at least historically. The Zuni reportedly collected turquoise from the Cerrillos Hills (Ferguson and Hart 1985; Hart 1984; Riley 1975), so it is likely that they were aware of the Cerrillos lead and copper deposits as well. Galena was reportedly obtained from the Sandia Mountains by a particular Zuni religious society (Ferguson and Hart 1985; Hart 1995), and copper ores may have come from the San Francisco Peaks of northern Arizona (Hart 1995).

Although there is no direct evidence for Zuni use of Socorro area ore deposits, Ferguson and Hart (1985, Map 20) report that a major Zuni trail crossed the Magdalena Mountains to reach Piro villages along the Rio Grande. Riley and Manson (1983) state that copper minerals from the Jerome area were traded during prehistoric and historic times along a route that crossed the Zuni region (see also Ferguson and Hart 1985, Map 19).

HR ICP-MS METHODOLOGY

I used high resolution magnetic sector inductively-coupled plasma mass spectrometry (Hr ICP-MS) to identify the geographic sources of lead ores used to make Zuni glaze paints based on their stable lead isotope ratios. Because this method has not yet gained widespread use, I present a summary of sample preparation and instrumentation parameters. The reader is also referred to Baker and others (2006), Habicht-Mauche and others (2002), Huntley (2004), and Huntley and others (2007) for further details.

Sampling

I selected a sample of 283 sherds decorated with glaze paint from sites in the Pescado Basin, El Morro Valley, and Box S Pueblo. These sherds were drawn from a larger sample for which I had previously determined glaze chemical compositions (Chapters 2 and 4; Huntley 2004, Table 4.1). The primary selection criterion for lead isotope analysis was a sherd with a large area of glaze paint. My goal was to include a wide range of glaze chemical compositions as determined by the electron microprobe, while at the same time sampling as many different ceramic types as possible from as many archaeological contexts within a site as possible. For most sites, the sample size is 30 sherds or more; however, Box S and Mirabal have lead isotope data for fewer than 30 samples (Huntley 2004, Table 6.1).

I compared glaze isotope ratios with ore isotope ratios previously determined by Habicht-Mauche and others (2000; and with others 2002) as well as a few older published sources (Ewing 1979, Table 1; Slawson and Austin 1960, Table 2). The older studies used different mass-spectrometry procedures and presented average isotope values only for all samples combined from a particular district. I analyzed several additional ore samples as part of this research (Table 5.1). The combined ore lead isotope database contained 98 samples: 45 samples from the northern and southern Cerrillos Hills mines, 4 samples from the Montezuma Mine (Placitas district), 4 samples from the northern Manzano Mountains and southern Sandia Mountains (Tijeras or Albuquerque district), 13 samples from the Magdalena district, 2 samples from the North Magdalena district and 30 samples from the Hansonburg district (Sierra Oscura Mountains). Other researchers and I (Habicht-Mauche and others 2000; Habicht-

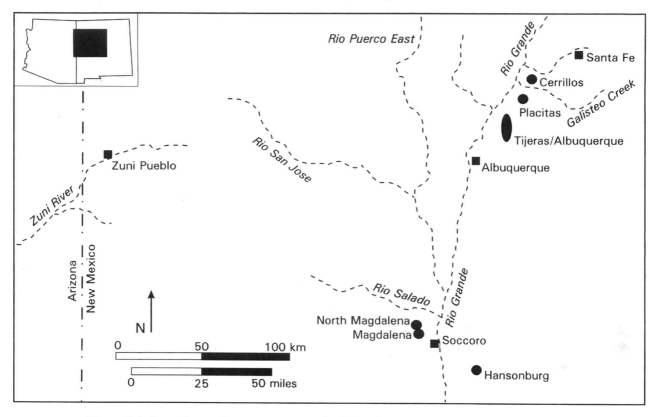

Figure 5.1. Locations of ore sources examined in this study; squares are modern towns.

Mauche and others 2002; Huntley and others 2007) have analyzed additional lead ore samples from throughout New Mexico, but only those that appear to correspond with the Zuni region glaze paint isotopic ratios are discussed here. I also exclude a few Cerrillos samples analyzed by Habicht-Mauche and others (2000) due to low lead concentrations or lack of statistical fit with the Cerrillos ore groups. Geographic locations of sampled ore sources are shown in Figure 5.1.

Sample Preparation

Approximately 2 mg of glaze or ore were removed from each specimen using a surgical stainless steel dissection blade and dissolved in one percent trace metal grade nitric acid (HNO_3). Samples were left in acid for approximately five months prior to dilution and analysis. Digested samples were then centrifuged so that undissolved material could be removed from the acid solutions prior to analysis, and the supernatant from each sample was poured into 30 ml bottles. Initially, sample and acid bottles were acid-cleaned (trace metal grade HNO_3) prior to sample preparation, but I discon-

Table 5.1. Lead Ore Samples Listed by Mining District

Mining District	Source	No. of Samples
Cerrillos North	Habicht-Mauche and others 2000; Habicht-Mauche and others 2002	21
Cerrillos South	Habicht-Mauche and others 2000; Habicht-Mauche and others 2002	24
Hansonburg	Huntley 2004; Ewing 1979; Slawson and Austin 1960	30
Magdalena	Huntley 2004; Habicht-Mauche and others 2000; Habicht-Mauche and others 2002; Ewing 1979; Slawson and Austin 1960	13
North Magdalena	Huntley 2004	2
Placitas	Habicht-Mauche and others 2000; Habicht-Mauche and others 2002	4
Tijeras/ Albuquerque	Huntley 2004; Habicht-Mauche and others 2000; Habicht-Mauche and others 2002	4
Total		*98*

tinued this practice once I determined that sample lead concentrations were so high as to completely mask any traces of lead contamination in new but unwashed sample bottles.

Prior to Hr ICP-MS lead isotope analysis, total lead concentrations were determined for each sample using a Perkins-Elmer inductively-coupled plasma optical emission spectrometer (ICP-OES). This step was needed to ensure that all samples had lead concentrations comparable to lead standards used in the isotopic analysis. Several glaze sample digestions had extremely low lead concentrations and were deemed not suitable for further lead isotope analysis. In most cases, these were glazes where copper was the most common ingredient. In other cases, the lead may have been bound up in silicates and not easily digested by the relatively weak acid solution. Following ICP-OES determination of lead concentrations, samples were diluted as necessary to concentrations below 1 part per million.

Instrumentation and Analysis Parameters

Stable lead isotope concentrations were determined using a Finnegan MAT ELEMENT high resolution magnetic sector inductively-coupled plasma mass spectrometer (Hr ICP-MS) at the Institute of Marine Sciences at the University of California, Santa Cruz (UCSC). In this type of analysis a liquid sample is pumped into a nebulizer, where it is converted into a fine aerosol. The aerosol is then transported and introduced into an argon plasma torch, which ionizes the injected sample. The ions generated by the plasma are then extracted through a series of cones into a mass spectrometer where they are separated based on their mass-to-charge ratio. Finally, an ion detector converts the ions into an electrical signal. This electronic signal is then translated into isotope concentrations by the data handling software.

The instrument was operated in analog mode and an autosampler was used to introduce aqueous sample dilutions into the plasma. Measured lead intensities were corrected for interference of ^{204}Hg with ^{204}Pb during analysis by monitoring ^{201}Hg to calculate a correction factor. All isotopic data also were dead time corrected using the instrument software (see Huntley 2004, Table C.2 for Hr ICP-MS operating conditions).

To assess Hr ICP-MS stability and standardize the isotopic data, an acid dissolution of standard NBS SRM 981 (common lead) was analyzed at the beginning, middle, and end of each batch of 24 samples. All isotopic ratios for glazes and ores were then standardized to the average NBS SRM 981 ratios for each sample batch. Blanks of one percent trace metal clean nitric acid were also run at the beginning, middle, and end of each sample batch. Blank levels were consistently below 0.05 percent of sample concentrations for ^{204}Pb and below 0.01 percent for ^{206}Pb, ^{207}Pb, and ^{208}Pb. Two procedural blanks containing the same nitric acid used to dilute the glaze and ore samples were also analyzed. These blanks were on average less than 0.01 percent of sample lead concentrations, confirming that any contaminant lead introduced during processing was insignificant.

Data Presentation and Statistics

Lead isotope data are typically plotted in two-dimensional space using various combinations of stacked plots of pairs of ratios (for example, $^{206}Pb/^{204}Pb$ and $^{207}Pb/^{204}Pb$ versus $^{208}Pb/^{204}Pb$). The plot provides a means of visually identifying ore source separation and correspondence between glazes and ore sources. Many researchers use bivariate plots to assign samples to ore source groups without further statistical analysis (for example, Brill and Wampler 1976; Habicht-Mauche and others 2000; Habicht-Mauche and others 2002; Huntley and others 2007; Wilson and others 2006). However, opinions vary as to which are the most appropriate ratios to plot. Since ^{206}Pb, ^{207}Pb, and ^{208}Pb isotopes are normalized to ^{204}Pb in geochronology and in characterizing lead ores (Gulson 1986), these isotopes are often presented over ^{204}Pb. Most researchers agree that it is important to examine all of the ratios and provide plots for the ratios that best illustrate group separation (Sayre and others 1992). In figures presented in this chapter I show ratios of ^{206}Pb, ^{207}Pb, and ^{208}Pb over ^{204}Pb because these plots provide the best visual representation of ore source separation and linear trends in the sample data.

Some researchers (for example, Gale and Stos-Gale 1993; Sayre and others 1992) recommend using stepwise discriminant function analysis to generate statistical probabilities for sample membership in ore source groups, but the small number of ore sources for all but the Cerrillos deposits precludes the use of this technique for the present study. Moreover, discriminant analysis assumes that each case belongs to one or more distinct groups present within a given dataset, that groups are similar in overall size and shape in multivariate space, and that all possible groups are represented in the dataset (Baxter 1994: 186, 197). These assumptions are unwarranted in the case of lead isotope data. For this reason I rely on visual examination of multiple bivariate plots with regression lines and 95% confidence ellipses for ore groups (where appropriate) in assigning glaze paint samples to ore source groups.

ORE SOURCE GROUPS

Figure 5.1 shows isotope ratios for ore samples listed in Table 5.1 (see Huntley 2004, Table C.3 for average isotopic ratios for each group of ore samples from a particular source). As this figure indicates, multiple samples from each source tend to plot as elongated, flattened ellipses with characteristic slopes, known as "evolution lines," which reflect the parent composition and geochemical history of each ore source. Because the Cerrillos North and Cerrillos South source groups have similar isotopic ratios, regression lines and 95 percent confidence ellipses are drawn for them as a combined group in this figure. Sample sizes for all other groups are too small to draw confidence ellipses, so ellipses drawn around these source groups enclose all of the analyzed ore samples for a particular source. I have not drawn a confidence ellipse or regression line for the North Magdalena group, which is represented by only two ore samples. One of the Magdalena points represents averages for nine samples (Ewing 1979).

Figure 5.2 shows that lead ores from some mining districts, such as Albuquerque and Hansonburg, cluster closely together and are easily distinguished from other source groups. Several source groups, however, partially overlap with one another. In the top plot in Figure 5.2, for example, the Cerrillos North and Cerrillos South samples are represented by the large group of overlapping solid and open circles on the far left side of the plot. Three Magdalena data points (represented by open rectangles plotted virtually on top of one another) overlap with the Cerrillos samples in the lower left corner of the plot; two other Magdalena samples plot on the right side of the plot. Samples from the two source groups do, however, typically plot along regression lines with different slopes (Fig. 5.2 upper plot).

Some overlap in the isotopic compositions of the Cerrillos and Magdalena ore deposits is not all that surprising considering that these two districts are similar in geologic age and depositional context (as indicated to me in 2002 by Virgil Leuth). For this reason I exercise caution when assigning glaze paints to ore sources.

Stacked bivariate plots facilitate comparisons between ore source groups and glaze paint samples. In Figure 5.3, isotopic ratios for St. Johns Polychrome glaze paints are plotted along with regression lines for ore source groups as they are first shown in Figure 5.2 (see Huntley 2004, Table C.4, for sample isotope data). In these and subsequent figures the upper plot is an enlarged view of the group of points enclosed by the rectangle in the lower plot (additional plots are in Huntley 2004, Appendix C).

For simplicity, I have omitted all ellipses except the Cerrillos 95 percent confidence ellipse and have not plotted individual Cerrillos ore samples. As Figure 5.3 indicates, most of the St. Johns glazes (27 of 35 samples) cluster on the lower left side of the plot. The eight St. Johns Polychrome sherds not in this cluster share one or more of the following attributes: they are from late contexts (n = 5), they have unusual interior or exterior design motifs (n = 4), or they may be classified as late St. Johns transitional to Heshotauthla Polychrome (n = 3).

The most striking difference in the isotope plot of Heshotauthla Polychrome (Fig. 5.4) and Kwakina Polychrome (Fig. 5.5) is that for these later types many more glazes are now distributed along an evolution line that appears to correspond with the Magdalena, Hansonburg, and possibly Albuquerque lead ores. However, the glaze paints do not exhibit the same groupings seen in the plot of ore samples alone (Fig. 5.2). Many overlap with the groups of ore samples, but many also plot in areas between ore source groups, perhaps due to mixing of ores from multiple sources to make glaze paints.

There are several reasons why assignment of glaze paints to ore sources must be made with some caution. First, since some of the Magdalena ore samples have been shown to overlap with the Cerrillos ore samples, it is difficult to resolve these two source groups. Preliminary research by Habicht-Mauche (unpublished data), using thermal ionization mass spectrometry (TIMS), suggests that combined Pb and Sr isotope analyses may provide a way to isotopically segregate the Cerrillos and Magdalena ore sources. Second, the small sample size for most of the ore sources makes the definition of group isotopic parameters tentative. A larger sample of southern ores may eventually allow us to better resolve the Cerrillos and Magdalena sources. Finally, I cannot rule

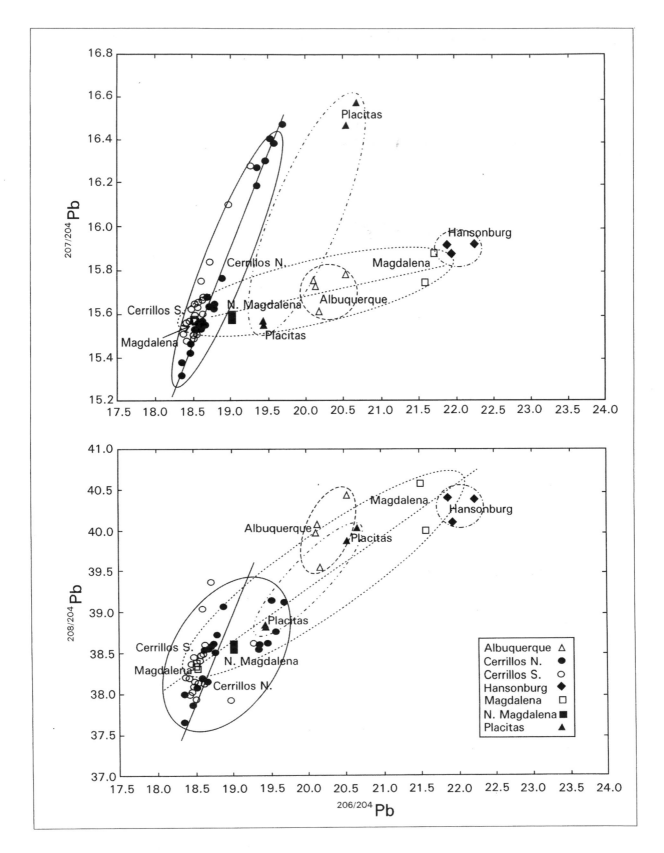

Figure 5.2. Plot of ore source lead isotope ratios over [206/204]Pb.

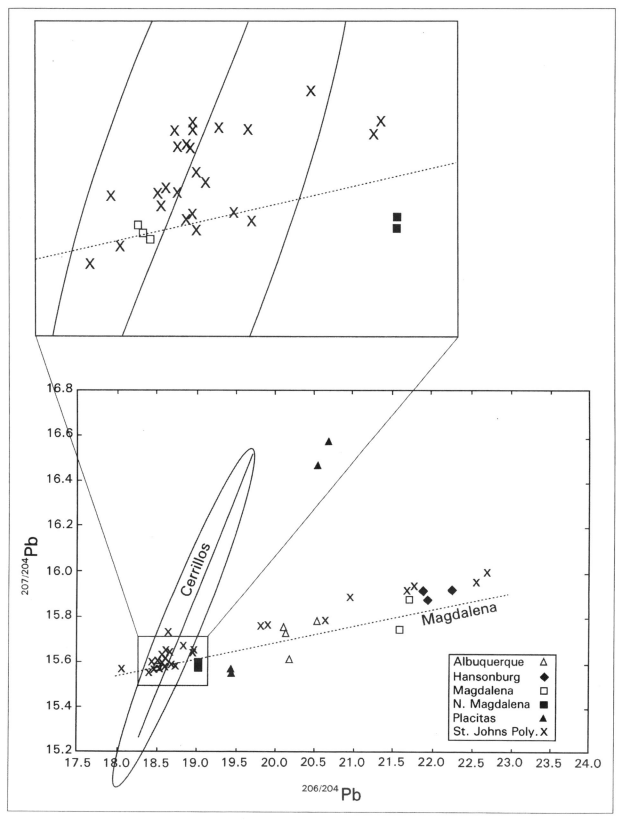

Figure 5.3. Plot of St. Johns Polychrome lead isotope ratios ($^{207/204}$Pb vs. $^{206/204}$Pb). Top plot is area denoted by rectangle in bottom plot.

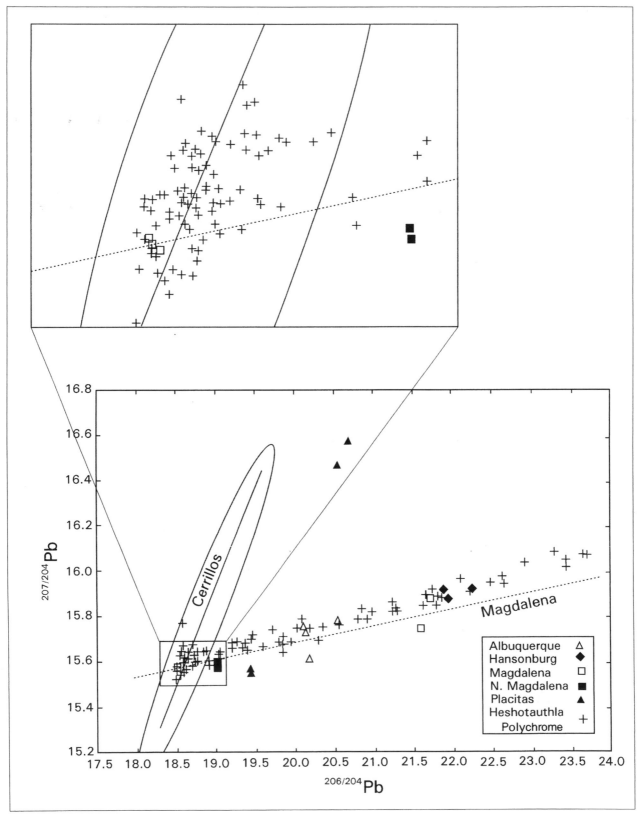

Figure 5.4. Plot of Heshotauthla Polychrome lead isotope ratios ($^{207/204}$Pb vs. $^{206/204}$Pb). Top plot is area denoted by rectangle in bottom plot.

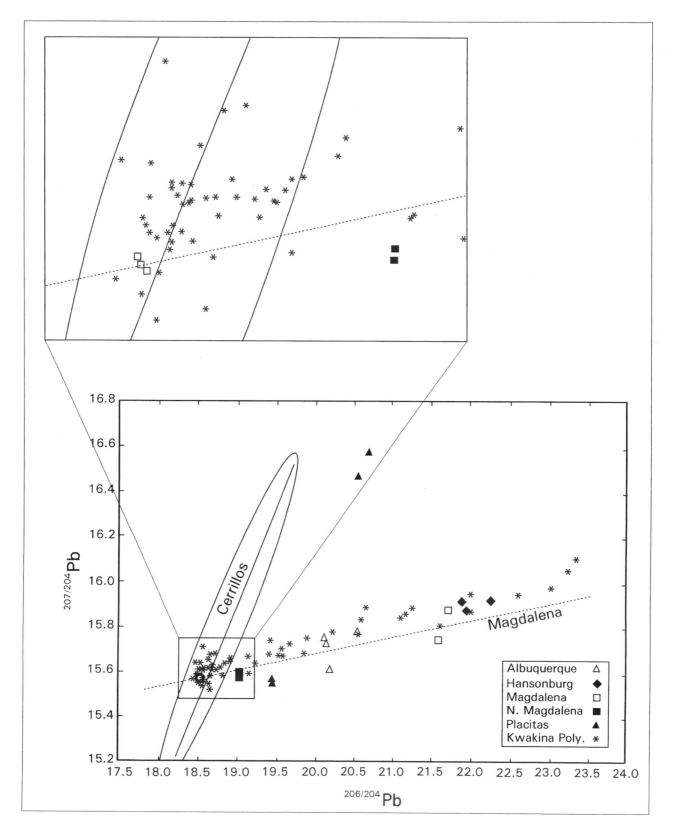

Figure 5.5. Plot of Kwakina Polychrome lead isotope ratios ($^{207/204}$Pb vs. $^{206/204}$Pb). Top plot is area denoted by rectangle in bottom plot.

Table 5.2. Ceramic Type Frequencies by Ore Source (All Sites Combined)

Ceramic Type	Ore Source (Count)				
	Cerrillos	Hanson-burg	Magda-lena	Indeter-minate	*Total*
St. Johns Polychrome	15	2	12	6	*35*
Heshotauthla Polychrome	37	3	69	30	*139*
Kwakina Poly.	18	2	32	23	*75*
Total	*70*	*7*	*113*	*59*	*249*

Table 5.3. Distribution of Ore Sources Among Compositional Groups

	Glaze Compositional Group (Column %)			
	1 (high Pb)	2 (high Mn)	3 (low Pb)	Total
Ore Source (n:	141	16	81	*238*)
Cerrillos	24.1%	31.3%	33.3%	27.7%
Hansonburg	2.8%	-	3.7%	2.9%
Magdalena	48.2%	43.8%	42.0%	45.8%
Indeterminate	24.8%	25.0%	21.0%	23.5%

out the possibility that some of the glazes were made from other sources that I did not sample. Bearing in mind these caveats, Table 5.2 presents probable ore source group classifications for glaze paint samples by ceramic type. Because of the lack of appropriate statistical techniques that can be used to group glaze samples, I relied on visual examination of multiple bivariate plots of isotope ratios, comparing each glaze paint sample with ore source regression lines and confidence intervals. Source determination for some samples was relatively easy, but a number of samples (n = 59) fell close to more than one regression line.

As Table 5.2 shows, slightly more St. Johns Polychrome glazes are attributed to Cerrillos ores (15 of 35 samples) than to other ore sources. Although Cerrillos ores continued to be used for Kwakina Polychrome and Heshotauthla Polychrome glazes, these types exhibited an increase in the utilization of Magdalena ores. For Heshotauthla Polychrome versus St. Johns Polychrome, differences in the relative distributions of Cerrillos and Magdalena ores were statistically significant ($p = .05$, $X^2 = 3.85$, 1 degree of freedom). Differences between St. Johns Polychrome and Kwakina Polychrome were not statistically significant ($p = .10$, $X^2 = 2.74$, 1 d.f.), nor were differences between Heshotauthla Polychrome and Kwakina Polychrome ($p = .89$, $X^2 = .02$, 1 d.f.).

Glazes attributed to ores from the Hansonburg mining district were much less common in general and were not distributed differently among ceramic types. Fifty-nine glaze samples (6 St. Johns Polychrome, 30 Heshotauthla Polychrome and 23 Kwakina Polychrome) could not be placed into a single source group. Most of these samples were attributed to either Cerrillos or Magdalena ores. A few plotted near the Albuquerque or Placitas samples for one or more pairs of isotope ratios,

but also fell close to the regression line for Magdalena ores.

ORE SOURCES AND GLAZE RECIPES

A comparison of glaze paint compositions (Chapter 4) with probable ore sources indicated that high lead and low lead paints were not strongly patterned by ore source. As shown in Table 5.3, the distribution of ore sources among glaze paint compositional groups 1, 2, and 3 was similar. Nearly half (48.2%) of all glazes in Group 1 were attributed to Magdalena ores and approximately 24 percent were likely made from Cerrillos ores. Just under 3 percent were from Hansonburg ores and 24.8 percent were of indeterminate ore source. The proportions of Cerrillos ores were higher and the percentages of Magdalena ores lower in both Groups 2 and 3, but the chance of Magdalena and Cerrillos ore sources being randomly distributed this differently or more differently in compositional groups 2 and 3 is nearly 20% based on Fisher's Exact test ($p = 0.18$).

One possible explanation for the isotopic (that is, lead source) similarities between some of the high copper (Group 3) and high lead (Group 1) glaze paints is that potters used copper ores containing minor amounts of lead impurities as a major ingredient in many of the high copper glazes. Lead and copper occur together within many Southwestern ore deposits, including the Cerrillos deposits (Disbrow and Stoll 1957: 49–50; Giles 1991: 64), and geologically associated copper and lead ores will typically bear the same lead isotope fingerprints (Stos-Gale 1992). Thus, if potters initially exploited Cerrillos copper ores for high copper paints and then switched to Cerrillos lead ores for high lead paints, the lead isotope signatures in the two paint recipes would have been similar. Potters likely mixed lead ores from several different sources, complicating the isotopic signatures even further. This mixing effect accounts for much of the isotopic variability that occurred in the sampled glaze paints, and mixing may also help to explain the lack of correspondence between glaze recipes and ore sources. (For another example of this phenomenon, see Wolf and others 2003.)

Mixing of ores from different sources to make glaze paints seems particularly likely because the ore sources that appear to have been used most commonly by Zuni region potters were several days distant by foot. Whether Zuni potters visited the Cerrillos and Magdalena area mines themselves or acquired galena through trade with villages near ore deposits, materials from various sources were probably stockpiled and used as needed. Stockpiled galena from different sources would have been visually indistinguishable. Habicht-Mauche and others (2000) argue that such stockpiling and mixing of ores from different Cerrillos district mines explains the isotopic variability existing in glaze paints on pottery from Galisteo Basin pueblos, and Huntley and others (2007) propose a similar phenomenon for the Salinas pueblos.

INTERCLUSTER AND INTERPUEBLO PATTERNS OF ORE UTILIZATION

Table 5.4 shows the distribution of ore source groups by pueblo cluster and individual pueblo. As the table indicates, glaze paints likely to have been made from Magdalena ores are more common than glaze paints made from Cerrillos or Hansonburg ores at nearly all sampled sites. A Fisher's Exact test on the distribution of Cerrillos versus Magdalena glazes in the El Morro Valley versus Pescado Basin sites produces a two-tailed probability of 0.87. Thus, there is a high probability that ore sources were not utilized differently between these two locations. Mirabal seems to have more Cerrillos glazes (8 of 16 samples) than other El Morro Valley sites, perhaps due to its relatively early assemblage. However, a series of Fisher's Exact tests comparing Mirabal to the other three El Morro Valley sites indicates that the probability of patterning at least this strong occurring if the variables are independent is between 20 percent and 35 percent, so I hesitate to attach much significance to this pattern.

El Morro Valley sites also have more glazes attributed to Hansonburg ores (6 of 159 samples) than do sites in other parts of the Zuni region. In fact, Box S

Table 5.4. Ore Source by Pueblo and Pueblo Cluster

| Pueblo/ Pueblo Cluster | Ore Source (Row %) | | | | |
	Cerrillos	Hanson- burg	Magda- lena	Indeter- minate	*Total Count*
Atsinna	23%	6%	49%	22%	*51*
Cienega	31%	6%	46%	17%	*35*
Mirabal	50%	–	37%	13%	*16*
Pueblo de los Muertos	25%	2%	40%	33%	*57*
El Morro Valley Subtotal	28%	4%	44%	24%	*159*
Heshotauthla	25%	2%	51%	22%	*51*
Lower Pescado Village	32%	–	44%	24%	*34*
Pescado Basin Subtotal	28%	1%	49%	22%	*85*
Box S Pueblo	20%	–	40%	40%	*5*
Total Percent	28%	3%	45%	24%	*100%*
Total Count	70	7	113	59	*249*

Pueblo and Lower Pescado Village have no glaze paints made from Hansonburg ores (in the case of Box S, perhaps because its relatively early assemblage predates regular use of southern ore sources), and only 1 of 51 glaze samples from Heshotauthla Pueblo is attributed to the Hansonburg source. However, Fisher's Exact tests on the distribution of Magdalena versus Hansonburg and Cerrillos versus Hansonburg ores for the El Morro Valley and Pescado Basin produce identical two-tailed probabilities of 0.42, indicating the probability of obtaining differences at least this marked (given the marginal totals) by chance is high.

Both ore source data and ceramic production source data (Chapter 3) are available for a subset of the total lead isotope dataset (n = 78). These samples are tabulated in Table 5.5, which indicates that ceramic samples from most production sources had glaze paints made from a variety of ore sources. However, a larger proportion of glazes on vessels from the El Morro Valley production zone (67%) was made with ores from the Magdalena district than glazes on vessels from other production zones (36% from the Pescado Basin, 25% from the Southwest and none from the North). Based on Fisher's Exact test, differences as great or greater than those observed between the El Morro and Pescado

Table 5.5. Ore Source by Production Source

Production Source	Ore Source (Row %)			
	Cerrillos	Hanson-burg	Magda-lena	Indeter-minate
El Morro (n = 15)	13%	-	67%	20%
Pescado (n = 55)	33%	2%	36%	29%
North (n = 4)	25%	-	-	75%
Southwest (n = 4)	25%	-	25%	50%
Total (n = 78)	*28%*	*1%*	*41%*	*30%*

NOTE: The table is not broken down into early and late contexts due to the small sample size.

Basin production sources are fairly unlikely to have occurred at random (two-tailed p = 0.09). Thus, I conclude that El Morro Valley potters utilized ores from the Magdalena district more often than did potters in other parts of the Zuni region.

Results based on isotopic sourcing of glaze paints from the Pueblo IV Zuni region indicated that potters used several different resources from distant ore deposits to make glaze paints. Difficulty in assigning many glaze paint samples to ore source groups may be due to several factors, including insufficient sampling of ore sources that were actually used prehistorically, isotopic overlap of some sampled ore sources, and mixing of lead ores stockpiled from multiple sources to make glaze paints. There is no way to evaluate the first possibility without additional sampling of other known ore sources. As for the second possibility, this research has shown that lead ores from the Magdalena mining district may be variable and that some lead ores from this district are difficult to distinguish from Cerrillos ores. Systematic sampling and isotopic characterization of ore deposits from the Magdalena district might resolve this issue. However, I also think that it is likely that much of the ambiguity in the Zuni lead isotope data

is the result of potters mixing lead ores from multiple sources to make glaze paints.

The observed patterns of ore resource utilization suggest long-distance social ties that crossed regional boundaries and traditionally defined culture areas. Although I cannot rule out the possibility that Pueblo IV Zuni region potters used resources that are not represented in my ore sample, many of the sampled glaze paints appear to have been made using ores from the Cerrillos Hills, particularly for the earliest glaze decorated type, St. Johns Polychrome. More frequently, glazes on later types of vessels were made using ores from sources located in the southern part of the Rio Grande Valley, although this pattern is not uniform throughout the region. In particular, the data suggest that El Morro Valley potters utilized ores from the Magdalena district more often than did potters from other parts of the Zuni region. I interpret this observation as an indication that residents of the cluster of El Morro Valley pueblos occasionally participated in different interaction networks compared with the rest of the Zuni region.

It is perhaps not surprising that Zuni region potters used Cerrillos deposits because they were reportedly a source for copper and turquoise in historic times (Ferguson and Hart 1985: 49). What is surprising is that the isotope data indicate regular, sustained contact between the Western and Eastern Pueblo regions dating at least as early as the late A.D. 1200s. Production of Rio Grande Glaze Ware began in the early 1300s at pueblos such as San Marcos in the Galisteo Basin, and by the mid–1300s this pueblo was supplying large amounts of glaze-decorated pottery to other Rio Grande villages (Shepard 1942). If Galisteo Basin pueblos exercised control over Cerrillos ores beginning in the early 1300s (Nelson and Habicht-Mauche 2006), Zuni region potters probably found these ores more difficult to obtain. As a result, potters may have turned to alternative sources more frequently.

CHAPTER SIX

A Multiscalar Perspective on Production, Exchange, and Pueblo IV Zuni Regional Organization

Like all aspects of human behavior, social interaction within the Pueblo IV Zuni region was undoubtedly a complex, multifaceted phenomenon. The archaeological record and the ceramic data I have presented capture only part of this complexity. Nevertheless, evidence for decorated and utility ware production and exchange, development of glaze recipes, use of color on ancestral Zuni glaze-decorated vessels, and lead ore utilization draws attention to three levels of interaction: within clusters of nucleated pueblos, among pueblo clusters, and with the larger social landscape beyond the Zuni region. Interactions at each of these three scales likely occurred simultaneously and varied in intensity through time. For the Zuni region, the organizational parameters of nucleated pueblos, pervasive regional population movement, and longstanding differences in occupational histories among pueblo clusters, discussed in Chapter 1, introduced an element of instability into everyday social life that resulted in the constant restructuring of interpersonal interactions at overlapping and shifting scales. I propose that intercluster integration, possibly in the form of alliances forged in the context of integrative ritual, was a pervasive concern for Zuni region residents, particularly those living in the El Morro Valley. This concern for integration may be attributed, at least in part, to the shorter occupational history of the El Morro Valley compared with the central Zuni region.

BOUNDARIES AND INTERACTION: A MATTER OF SCALE

The various kinds of data presented in Chapters 3 through 5 imply different behaviors interpreted as evidence for particular scales of interaction in the Pueblo IV Zuni region (Table 6.1). Zuni region potters participated in overlapping spheres of interaction, or communities of practice. These communities of practice structured the technological and stylistic choices that potters made in their daily production activities. Pottery consumers (not just potters, but all individuals with access to their products) exchanged utility ware and decorated ware in various contexts that signaled a different range of social transactions.

Figure 6.1 is a representation of my interpretation of intersecting interaction networks within the Pueblo IV Zuni region. In this figure, circles represent individual nucleated pueblos. As the dashed circles enclosing pueblo clusters indicate, I propose that social transactions among individuals within pueblo clusters define major interaction spheres. Rather than clearly demarcated boundaries, these spheres form permeable membranes. Dashed arrows linking clusters indicate social interactions that occurred less frequently among residents of different pueblo clusters. Additional arrows extending away from pueblo clusters indicate interregional interactions, which probably also occurred less frequently and with less intensity than interactions within and among pueblo clusters. Of necessity, the figure is idealized in that it shows only those pueblos included in my sample. It remains to be discovered where other Zuni region pueblos might fit into the diagram. Below I discuss the behaviors and ceramic evidence for each level of interaction: among pueblos in the same cluster (local interaction spheres), among different pueblo clusters (regional alliances), and long-distance interactions.

Local Interaction Spheres

It appears that much of everyday social discourse within the Pueblo IV Zuni region occurred among residents of nucleated pueblos and their neighbors

Table 6.1. Summary of Evidence and Behavioral Implications for Different Scales of Interaction

Primary Scale of Interaction	Behavior	Data
Local	1. Consistent use of local resources defining cluster-level potters' communities of practice	1. INAA sourcing
	2. Differential adoption of high lead recipe among pueblo clusters	2. Glaze compositions
	3. Differences in application of conventional color schemes	3. White slip colors
Regional	1. Widely shared basic Zuni region glaze recipe	1. Glaze compositions
	2. Shared general color scheme conventions for red-slipped bowls used and exchanged in formal contexts	2. Red slip colors
	3. Moderate west-east decorated ware exchange (formal contexts) among Pueblo clusters; infrequent utility ware exchange (informal contexts) among pueblo clusters	3. INAA sourcing
Long-distance	1. Lead ore acquisition from Cerrillos and Magdalena areas	1. Lead isotope sourcing
	2. Participation in Southwestern Regional Cult (Crown 1994) or other pan-Southwestern socioreligious system	2. Use of polychrome color scheme and glaze paint

within pueblo clusters. The INAA data indicate that ceramic compositional groups reflect production zones that generally correspond to the geographic locations of pueblo clusters. Although there is some degree of overlap in available clay resources between the El Morro Valley and Pescado Basin, Zuni region potters apparently consistently selected clay resources that were nearest to the pueblo or pueblo cluster in which they resided. Thus, ceramic paste compositions reflect potters' communities of practice that were defined at a relatively small scale, perhaps within 10 km (6.2 miles) or less.

In addition, El Morro Valley and Pescado Basin potters frequently applied white slips with subtle hue differences to Kwakina Polychrome bowl interiors. Although this practice may reflect, in part, the geographic distribution of slip clay resources, it may also indicate an attempt to distinguish Kwakina Polychrome bowls made in the Pescado Basin from those made in other parts of the Zuni region.

Certain aspects of glaze paint compositional data also suggest that potters' interactions were largely concentrated within pueblo clusters. Specifically, potters from pueblos in the Pescado Basin cluster appear to have adopted a high lead glaze recipe more completely and earlier than did potters in the El Morro Valley or Jaralosa clusters. This activity may be an indication that

interactions among potters were most regular and intense within pueblo clusters, with less frequent interactions and information sharing among potters residing in different clusters.

Regional Alliances

Ceramic production and exchange data, along with settlement patterns and other archaeological evidence, contradict expectations for hierarchical alliances characterized by economic specialization and highly developed exchange networks. Instead, the data are more consistent with nonhierarchical alliances. El Morro Valley residents faced a unique set of social circumstances stemming from the pressures associated with integrating diverse populations within the walls of nucleated pueblos, as well as the challenges and opportunities provided by residence in a portion of the Zuni region only sparsely occupied prior to the thirteenth century. Under these circumstances, El Morro Valley residents may have attempted to mediate social uncertainty by forming alliances with populations in other portions of the Zuni region and elsewhere. A possible avenue for alliance formation was within the realm of integrative ritual events hosted at El Morro Valley pueblos. Ceramic exchange transactions and exchanges of information were likely components of those events.

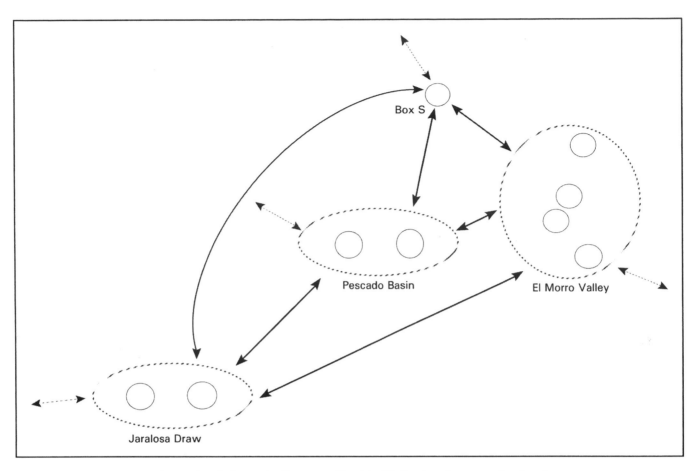

Figure 6.1. Schematic diagram of Pueblo IV Zuni region organizational scale. Circles indicate pueblos; dashed lines indicate pueblo clusters.

Potters' communities of practice were largely defined by residence in a particular nucleated pueblo or pueblo cluster, but there is evidence these communities often extended beyond these boundaries. Adoption of a high lead glaze recipe throughout the Zuni region implies a degree of communication that can only be attributed to face-to-face interaction. As discussed in Chapter 4, although Zuni glazes are probably not so complex as to require formal instruction in glaze preparation, some degree of information sharing among potters would have been necessary to reproduce the basic recipe and proper firing conditions required to create a vitreous paint. Assuming that women were the primary producers of glaze-decorated pottery, much of this interaction was among women. However, if matrilocal residence was the norm in prehistory as it was for the historic Zuni, then women were probably not moving around extensively. Thus, the relatively rapid spread of the high lead glaze paint recipe is not likely the result of potters relocating

to other pueblos. It is more likely that women maintained social ties with relatives living in other pueblos, and potters' communities of practice probably often included a number of related women from multiple pueblos, including the wives, sisters, and daughters of male kin.

Potters throughout the Zuni region consistently used particular red slip hues on St. Johns Polychrome and Heshotauthla Polychrome bowls during the Pueblo IV period. This pattern may mean that potters adhered to widely held conventions concerning the use of background colors on red-slipped bowls. Furthermore, regional uniformity in slip color may be related to use of glaze-decorated bowls in multipueblo integrative ritual activities. Consistent use of particular red slip colors throughout the Zuni region may have involved shared access to resources, but it also may indicate that potters conformed to widely shared conventions concerning the use of background colors on polychrome pottery. As with shared glaze recipes, conformity in this particular aspect of production implies a degree of region-wide communication among potters within a larger community of practice.

Moderate levels of west to east decorated ware exchange indicate that some interaction occurred among pottery consumers residing in different pueblo clusters, and this interaction likely occurred in formal contexts, such as integrative ceremonial events. El Morro Valley residents, in particular, appear to have obtained large numbers of nonlocal decorated bowls from other portions of the Zuni region. In contrast to the El Morro Valley, the movement of pottery into the Pescado Basin and the Box S area involved very small amounts of utility ware as well as some decorated ware. Informal utility ware exchanges may often have been facilitated by interactions among women, including visits to kin, as has been documented for some Melanesian societies. Among the Kalinga of the Philippines, for example, potters (mostly female) visit kin and long-term trading partners living in neighboring villages, exchanging their wares primarily for food (Stark 1992).

In the Southwest, many scholars postulate relatively fluid, informal, and largely nonhierarchical social relationships among individual pueblos for the purposes of mitigating subsistence risk, minimizing intergroup conflict (for example, Habicht-Mauche 1993; LeBlanc 2000; Spielmann 1994), or fulfilling ritual needs (W. Graves 1996, 2002; Potter 1997). A range of terms is used to describe these social relationships, including complex tribes (Habicht-Mauche 1993), confederacies (Spielmann 1994), alliances (LeBlanc 2000, 2001), or complementary pairs (Potter 1997; Potter and Perry 2000). Some researchers conceive of late prehistoric and protohistoric Pueblo intergroup relationships as more hierarchically organized and based on interactions among unequal polities (for example, Lightfoot and Upham 1989; F. Plog 1985; F. Plog and Upham 1983; Stone 1992; Upham and Plog 1986; Wilcox 1981, 1991). A few have gone so far as to suggest that regional polities were managed by small groups of elites residing in regional political centers (Upham 1982; Upham and Reed 1989).

The idea that Pueblo IV regions were characterized by centralized, hierarchical political entities has been criticized on a number of fronts. On a methodological level, the identification of elite-based control over ceramic exchange networks is largely based on the erroneous assumption that smaller sites lacking poly-chrome pottery are contemporaneous with large pueblos (Duff 1999, 2002). Furthermore, I am unaware of any undisputed archaeological evidence for elite managers at any Pueblo IV pueblo. For the Zuni region in particular, the settlement pattern data presented in Chapter 1 provide no clear evidence for a "central" pueblo. In contrast, there are several site size modes and these modes vary throughout the course of the Pueblo IV period (see Huntley and Kintigh 2004). Hierarchical regional organization also implies management of long-distance exchange, or at least unequal access to long-distance social relationships and items acquired via long-distance exchange. Region-wide similarity in the distributions of glaze paints made with lead ores from distant sources contradicts this expectation. The most convincing line of evidence against hierarchical regional organization for the Zuni region, however, is the lack of compelling evidence for centralized pottery production and distribution (Duff 1999, 2002). On the contrary, there is evidence for localized production (at least at the level of pueblo clusters) and moderate levels of exchange.

This research also provided little evidence to support the role of conflict as a driving force behind regional settlement patterns and the formation of interpueblo alliances (LeBlanc 1998, 1999, 2000, 2001; Wilcox 1981, 1991; Wilcox and Haas 1994; Wilcox and others 2000). A complete evaluation of the role of conflict in the Pueblo Southwest is beyond the scope of this study, but some of the particulars of LeBlanc's assessment of the prevalence and intensity of violent conflict within the Zuni region require a rebuttal. His interpretation of burned rooms universally as evidence for conflict, for example, fails to sufficiently rule out other possible explanations for burning (LeBlanc 2001). More importantly, I disagree with the uncritical assumption, inherent in LeBlanc's (2001) argument, that violent attacks against Pueblo de los Muertos and other El Morro Valley pueblos were perpetrated by individuals from other pueblos within the same cluster or by individuals from other pueblo clusters within the Zuni region. To begin to really understand the nature and intensity of conflict in the American Southwest, we must take into consideration exactly who we think is involved, rather than framing conflict in abstract terms. The data in this book provide no clear indications that individual pueblos or pueblo clusters maintained clear social identities that would have resulted in obvious distinctions between insiders (us) versus outsiders (them). As

Bernardini (2002, 2005) similarly argues for the Homol'ovi and Anderson Mesa regions, regional social diversity and overlapping spheres of interaction linking nucleated villages in different pueblo clusters provide evidence against any predisposition toward organized conflict.

Several key features, including the fact that Zuni is a language isolate (Hill 2001), the fact that the region has had continuous settlement and high population density since at least A.D. 1050, and the present-day Zuni perception of direct cultural affiliation with the Zuni region lead Duff (2002: 172–173) to characterize the Zuni region as "historically persistent." This historical persistence, Duff argues, resulted in an inflexible social structure typified by rigid rules. I do not disagree with Duff's general argument, but I do think that it is more applicable to some portions of the Zuni region than others. El Morro Valley residents, in particular, may have attempted to mediate social uncertainty by forming alliances with people residing in more demographically (and perhaps socially) stable portions of the Zuni region. In the late A.D.1200s and early 1300s, the population of the El Morro Valley increased dramatically compared to earlier time periods and probably even surpassed the population of the Pescado Basin and other "core" areas with historically dense occupations (Chapter 1; Kintigh and others 2006). Newly constructed El Morro Valley pueblos probably incorporated diverse populations, including a large number of newcomers to the region, who likely found themselves in an uncertain social and political landscape. It is possible that such uncertainty was based, in part, on fear of possible violence against the relative newcomers, but I consider it more likely that social uncertainty was due to other factors, such as a desire to participate in emerging ritual systems that were centered in the Zuni region core area. Perhaps El Morro Valley pueblos lacked key components of the ritual system and tried to recruit outsiders to fill those roles (see Duff 2002: 182 for a similar argument applied to interregional interaction).

One mechanism for forming alliances was hosting events (feasts, dances, or ceremonies) attended by outsiders who brought with them glaze-decorated bowls that were eventually discarded at the El Morro Valley pueblos. Many ethnographic studies focus on the importance of public ritual events in negotiating intergroup social relationships (Hayden 1995; Rappaport 1968, 1979). Abbott (1996, 2000; Abbott and Walsh-Anduze 1995) noted that formalized exchanges of red

ware vessels among Classic Period Hohokam communities in the Phoenix Basin occurred within the context of public ceremonies (at ball courts or platform mounds) or trade fairs. Although the particulars of this archaeological case differ from the Pueblo IV Zuni region, the social processes may have been broadly similar.

In my sample, the two largest El Morro Valley sites, Pueblo de los Muertos and Atsinna, have a few more nonlocal decorated vessels than do Cienega and Mirabal pueblos. Whether this pattern indicates that Atsinna and Pueblo de los Muertos residents were more successful in forging intraregional alliances than the other two El Morro Valley pueblos or whether it is due to differences in INAA sample size, however, cannot be resolved at present. Notably, Potter (1997: 223) states that the Pueblo de los Muertos ceramic assemblage also contains disproportionate numbers of large cooking pots, a pattern that he attributes to that pueblo hosting frequent and elaborate feasts. Potter (1997; Potter and Perry 2000) also observes that all four El Morro Valley pueblos exhibit differences in faunal distributions that, ethnographically, are ritually significant. In particular, the faunal assemblages of Atsinna and Pueblo de los Muertos contain large numbers of raptors and perching birds, whereas Cienega and Mirabal contain more waterfowl (Potter and Perry 2000: 72). Potter (1997; Potter and Perry 2000) interprets these patterns as a result of intracluster ritual complementarity, specifically between pueblos with rectangular layouts (Pueblo de los Muertos and Atsinna) and those with oval layouts (Cienega and Mirabal). Unfortunately, this interpretation is based on small samples of identified wild birds at Atsinna (n = 4) and Mirabal (n = 16), with larger samples from Pueblo de los Muertos (n = 90) and Cienega (n = 43). Furthermore, Kintigh (2007; see also Potter 1997: 135–144, 173–174, 199–204) points out that wild bird bones are unevenly distributed across the excavated assemblages and that different types of deposits were sampled at various sites. Moreover, Cienega, the site with the largest number of waterfowl bones (n = 23), incorporates a large, standing water spring, and Mirabal, the other oval site, is less than 300 m away (Kintigh 2007). Clearly, relatively large numbers of waterfowl at these two pueblos could be due to the local environment.

Because glaze-decorated bowls were important in certain ritual contexts, if such rituals entailed complementary relationships among paired pueblos, one pueblo may have been responsible for providing glaze-decorated bowls as part of its ritual obligations. This situation seems especially likely if complementarity was asymmetrical (for example, a "mother" pueblo hosting a ritual event attended by a "daughter" pueblo). Exchanges of decorated pottery might also have been made in return for ceremonial services in particular contexts (see Ford 1972: 37 for some examples among the Tewa). Glaze-decorated bowls may have been regularly transported between complementary pueblos, but unfortunately my ceramic production and exchange data provided scant evidence for strong complementary relationships between pairs of nucleated pueblos. Perhaps the kinds of data collected did not provide the evidence needed to identify the ritual aspect of complementarity, or my focus on one particular type of material culture (pottery) did not identify complementary relationships. A larger INAA sample and a more detailed level of geological resolution might pinpoint ceramic production locations at the intracluster level and trace the movement of glaze-decorated bowls between complementary pairs of pueblos. Notwithstanding these issues, I suggest that ritual complementarity, if it did exist, need not have been restricted to pueblos within the same cluster. Social ties with pueblos outside of the El Morro Valley could also account for the differential distributions of varieties of large game that Potter (1997) and Potter and Perry (2000) propose for pairs of El Morro Valley pueblos.

Long-Distance Interaction

The Zuni region is often conceptualized as relatively isolated and inwardly focused during the Pueblo IV period. In contrast to the nearby Upper Little Colorado region, for example, Zuni region archaeological sites have yielded few examples of pottery types from other regions (Duff 1999, 2002; Kintigh 1985a), and items associated with long-distance exchange, such as shell and turquoise, are also rare. Isotope sourcing of glaze paints, however, indicates that Zuni region potters utilized a variety of ore deposits, many of which were located a few hundred kilometers away. Since gaining access to distant ore sources likely depended on establishing diverse, long-distance social connections, long-distance interaction may have been a much more important concern for the Pueblo IV Zuni region than has been previously recognized. Numerous glaze paints used to decorate St. Johns Polychrome and early Heshotauthla and Kwakina polychromes were made using ores

from mines in the Cerrillos Hills near Santa Fe, and interregional social connections were apparently strongest with the northern Rio Grande area during the early portion of the Pueblo IV period. Later in the Pueblo IV period, Zuni region residents intensified previously existing social networks with populations along the southern Rio Grande, increasing their use of lead ores from the Magdalena Mountains near Socorro. Although there are suggestions of regional variability in ore source utilization, potters from different Zuni region pueblos had access to the same range of ore sources, indicating that either everyone in the region shared access to the same long-distance social networks or that these networks were monopolized by a small number of individuals who controlled the regional distribution of ore resources.

Notably, the El Morro Valley pueblo cluster, by virtue of its location along major travel and trade routes that connected the central portion of the Zuni region with Ácoma and, eventually, with the Rio Grande Valley (Ferguson and Hart 1985, Map 20), was in a strategic position to take advantage of ore acquisition and information sharing. Pueblo ethnographies offer several examples of certain Pueblo groups serving as middlemen for long-distance exchange transactions. According to Ford (1972: 37–40), Santo Domingo traders exchanged marine shells and Mexican feathers they obtained from Zuni with Tewa groups. The role of Pecos Pueblo as a trade center during the protohistoric period is also well known (Riley 1975; Spielmann 1989; Wilcox 1981). Although there is no evidence to suggest that El Morro Valley residents directly controlled access to trails, formal exchanges of decorated ware may have been an expression of good will as travelers from the central and southern portions of the Zuni region passed through the El Morro Valley. In return, El Morro Valley residents may have been able to offer access to other resources, or perhaps to information, in exchange for glaze-decorated bowls. Several of the El Morro Valley pueblos included in this study are considered historically and culturally affiliated with the Ácoma region (Dittert 1998), and undoubtedly El Morro Valley residents played a role, during the Pueblo IV period, in Zuni-Ácoma interactions. It is also possible that El Morro Valley residents took the lead in establishing social and economic connections among the larger Zuni region and populations in the northern Rio Grande and Magdalena regions. Pottery is but one example of material culture that sheds light on these connections.

DIRECTIONS FOR FUTURE RESEARCH

Some specific questions suggested by this research might be addressed with additional studies, including methodological issues related specifically to the Zuni region and larger issues relevant to Southwestern prehistory. First, a more detailed understanding of variability in clay resources within particular formations present in the Zuni region is essential to refine the scale at which production and exchange can be examined. Such understanding can only be achieved through systematic chemical compositional analysis of clay samples. Barbara Mills has pursued such studies for the central part of the Zuni region, but the geological variability of other portions of the region has not been fully investigated.

An extensive program of Southwestern ore source sampling is also needed to establish a baseline for comparison with glaze paints. Until this work is accomplished, it will be difficult to compare patterns of ore resource utilization among regions. In addition, experimental studies are necessary to understand the complex relationships between glaze ingredients such as lead and copper with firing conditions and glaze colors.

We also need to more closely consider the relationships among Zuni region core pueblos and those in more peripheral areas. Although my research design included few pueblos from the extreme northern and southern portions of the region, the ceramic paste compositional data suggest that pueblos like Ojo Bonito and Spier 170 were only loosely connected with pueblos in the Pescado Basin and the El Morro Valley.

A related issue is where the boundaries of the Zuni region should really be drawn. Were these boundaries relatively rigid? Or were they more fluid as were social boundaries within the region? The social dynamics of the Zuni region cannot be fully understood without reference to the neighboring Ácoma region. Zuni and Ácoma clearly shared a cultural connection as shown by similar ceramic traditions. Archaeology and oral history suggest that this connection was strongest between Ácoma and the El Morro Valley pueblos. Exchange among El Morro Valley pueblos and pueblos in the Ácoma region would explain some of the compositional variability present in the INAA dataset and might account for many of the samples that could not be assigned to a particular Zuni region compositional group.

On a more substantive level, this study has implications for the ways archaeologists study leadership and power in ancestral Pueblo society, not only because it casts serious doubt on the notion of hierarchical or centralized political and economic entities, but also because it suggests alternative venues for the concentration of social power. This research raises the possibility that one avenue for the development of leadership in the Pueblo IV Zuni region was differential skill in the negotiation of both local and long-distance social connections that mitigated social stress, possibly within the realm of ritual-related events. An additional aspect of power is control over long-distance resources and negotiating the social transactions that acquiring those resources entailed.

Other researchers have noted that control over access to certain kinds of knowledge, particularly in the ritual realm, is one means by which social power is distributed within Pueblo society (Brandt 1980; W. Graves and Spielmann 2000; Potter 1998; Potter and Perry 2000). Considering the likely role of glaze-decorated bowls in integrative rituals that were part of pan-Southwestern religious transformations of the Pueblo IV period, the very act of producing glazes and glaze-decorated ceramics may have carried a certain amount of social power or prestige. What distinguishes glaze-decorated bowls from other pottery produced and used in domestic contexts is the lead and copper ores used to make the paints that decorated them. These ores usually were obtained from long distances and thus may have been considered rare or exotic, required some degree of specialized knowledge and technical skill to correctly manipulate, and were the same materials used in explicitly ritual and secretive contexts. A transformable raw material, such as lead ore, is considered more symbolically powerful if it is perceived as exotic (Helms 1993), as probably would have been the case for ores from distant sources. Transformation of powdered galena, an exotic material from the world outside of the boundaries of the Zuni region, into a vitreous paint may have represented an important form of specialized or esoteric knowledge. To the extent that potters controlled the transformation of exotic lead ores, this esoteric knowledge may have translated into social power.

Significantly, women may have wielded much of this social power in particular contexts. As Mills (2000: 335) points out, there likely was social value (in addition to possible economic value) attached to decorated bowls themselves in that they "might have been produced by a few but used by many in the construction of social identities." Moreover, women not only produced utility ware jars and decorated bowls used in public ritual contexts, but also likely prepared and served food consumed in such contexts (Crown 2000). Thus, both in the domestic and ritual realms, women may have gained status through their control over the preparation and serving of food using pottery they created.

There is some evidence to suggest, however, that control over the resources needed for glaze paint production was not exclusively in the hands of potters. Control over certain valued raw materials, such as turquoise, salt, and clay, has been documented elsewhere in the Pueblo Southwest (Ellis 1981). Although I do not directly equate pottery glazes with ritual paraphernalia, such as masks and kiva murals, it is worthwhile to note that a similar range of minerals is used in the creation of all these items. For ritual paraphernalia, use of these minerals carries certain proscriptions. In present-day Pueblo society, members of particular religious societies (usually men) often control access to precious minerals. Bunzel (1984) reports that members of Zuni medicine societies traditionally control access to mineral paints used to decorate Kachina masks, and ceremonies often accompany mask production. Restricted paints are commonly referred to as "valuable." Moreover, restricted access to lead ores might have been enforced by populations living near those sources (Habicht-Mauche and others 2000).

The potential for restricted access to the raw materials needed to make glaze paints, and perhaps even to the knowledge necessary to create them, raises the possibility that specialists controlled glaze paint manufacture. If these specialists were mobile, it would account for the adoption of high lead glazes throughout much of the Zuni region (perhaps even the spread of glaze paints throughout the northern Southwest), as well as for the increasing standardization in glaze paint recipes through time. Alternatively, these phenomena might be explained by widespread circulation of premade glaze paints produced in a limited number of locations (Nelson and Habicht-Mauche 2006).

Finally, the results of this study make it clear that archaeologists cannot ignore the role that long-distance interaction played in the Zuni region and the Pueblo IV Southwest in general. Zuni region populations apparently maintained longstanding ties to the northern Rio Grande and Socorro regions that have implications for large-scale population movement, regional settlement reorganization, and the development of a pan-Southwestern glaze horizon during the Pueblo IV and protohistoric periods. Glaze-decorated vessels first appeared along a corridor extending from the Mogollon Mountains on the southwest, through the Zuni and Ácoma regions, and east across the Rio Puerco of the East to the Albuquerque area, during a narrow window of time from around A.D. 1280 to 1320 (Cordell, personal communication, 2003; Eckert 2006). This rapid transmission of the technological knowledge needed to produce glaze paints is probably the result of face-to-face communications among potters from different parts of the northern Southwest, perhaps the result of population migration (Herhahn 2006).

Across the northern Southwest, the Pueblo IV period was a time during which new settlement and religious configurations developed. The Pueblo IV period also appears to have been a time when new social dynamics emerged, as regional populations negotiated social connections, established and blurred social boundaries, and defined social identities at many scales. This study suggests that social and economic conditions were different in the Pueblo IV Zuni region compared with other parts of the Southwest, such as the Hopi, Rio Grande, and Upper Little Colorado regions. In the Zuni region there is no evidence for the widespread economic specialization and production of glaze-decorated pottery for exchange that characterizes the Rio Grande region (Habicht-Mauche 1995; Spielmann 1998; Wilcox 1981). On the other hand, there is evidence for loosely connected, fluid alliances within the Zuni region organized in a way similar to Rio Grande confederacies (Spielmann 1994), albeit on a much smaller spatial scale.

The various lines of evidence presented in this volume indicate that Zuni region potters, and other individuals with access to the products of potters, used pottery to negotiate social relationships at different scales. Depending on the scale at which one looks, one might draw completely different conclusions concerning regional organization. Low levels of utility ware exchange among pueblo clusters suggest that individuals made a conscious effort to concentrate social interactions within individual pueblos or within pueblo clusters. Alliances among nucleated pueblos may have been formalized by exchange transactions involving decorated pottery, perhaps within the context of integrative rituals. Zuni region potters shared glaze paint recipes, as well as general styles of polychrome pottery decoration, that suggest broader regional communities of practice.

At the same time, use of polychrome decorative styles and of glaze paints signals participation in a pan-Southwestern socioreligious movement. Patterns of ore resource utilization suggest even wider social ties that transcended regional boundaries and traditionally defined culture areas. Thus, for people living in the Zuni region during the Pueblo IV period, social boundaries and interactions were permeable and defined at multiple scales. The challenge to archaeologists is to use material culture to disentangle complex and seemingly contradictory patterns of behavior. This research takes an important step in that direction.

References

Abbott, David R.
1996 Ceramic Exchange as a Strategy for Reconstructing Organizational Developments among the Hohokam. In "Interpreting Southwestern Diversity: Underlying Principles and Overarching Patterns," edited by Paul R. Fish and J. Jefferson Reid, pp. 147–158. *Arizona State University Anthropological Research Paper* 48. Arizona State University, Tempe.
2000 *Ceramics and Community Organization among the Hohokam.* University of Arizona Press, Tucson.

Abbott, David R., and Mary-Ellen Walsh-Anduze
1995 Temporal Patterns without Temporal Variation: The Paradox of Hohokam Redware Ceramics. In *Ceramic Production in the American Southwest*, edited by Barbara J. Mills and Patricia L. Crown, pp. 88–114. University of Arizona Press, Tucson.

Adams, E. Charles
1991 *The Origin and Development of the Pueblo Katsina Cult.* University of Arizona Press, Tucson.
2002 *Homol'ovi: An Ancient Hopi Settlement Cluster.* University of Arizona Press, Tucson.

Adams, E. Charles, and Andrew I. Duff
2004 Settlement Clusters and the Pueblo IV Period. In *The Protohistoric Pueblo World, A.D. 1275–1600*, edited by E. Charles Adams and Andrew I. Duff, pp. 3–16. University of Arizona Press, Tucson.
2004 [Editors] *The Protohistoric Pueblo World, A.D. 1275–1600.* University of Arizona Press, Tucson.

Adams, E. Charles, Miriam T. Stark, and Deborah S. Dosh
1993 Ceramic Distribution and Exchange: Jeddito Yellow Ware and Implication for Societal Complexity. *Journal of Field Archaeology* 20: 3–21.

Akright, Robert L.
1979 Geology and Mineralogy of the Cerrillos Copper Deposit, Santa Fe County, New Mexico. In *Guidebook to the 30th Field Conference, Santa Fe Country*, pp. 257–260. New Mexico Geological Society, Socorro.

Allen, James
1984 Pots and Poor Princes: A Multidimensional Approach to the Role of Pottery Trading in Coastal Papua. In *The Many Dimensions of Pottery*, edited by Sander E. van der Leeuw and Alison C.Pritchard, pp. 55–733. Albert Egges Van Giffen Instituut, Universiteit van Amsterdam, Amsterdam.

Al-Saa'd, Z.
2000 Technology and Provenance of a Collection of Islamic Copper-Based Objects as Found by Chemical and Lead Isotope Analysis. *Archaeometry* 42(1): 385–397.

Anderson, Orin J.
1987 *Geology and Coal Resources of the Atarque Lake 1:50,000 Quadrangle, New Mexico.* Geologic Map 61. New Mexico Bureau of Mines and Mineral Resources, Socorro.

Anderson, Orin J., and Charles H. Maxwell
1991 *Geology of the El Morro Quadrangle, Cibola County, New Mexico.* Geologic Map 72. New Mexico Bureau of Mines and Mineral Resources, Socorro.

Anyon, Roger
1987 Prehistoric Cultures. In *An Archaeological Reconnaissance of West-Central New Mexico: The Anasazi Monuments Project*, edited by Andrew P. Fowler, John R. Stein, and Roger Anyon, pp. 20–28. Report submitted to the New Mexico Office of Cultural Affairs, Historic Preservation Division, Santa Fe.

Arnold, Dean E.
1985 *Ceramic Theory and Cultural Process.* Cambridge University Press, Cambridge.

Arnold, Dean E., Hector Neff,
and Michael D. Glascock
2000 Testing Assumptions of Neutron Activation Analysis: Communities, Workshops and Paste Preparation in Yucatán, Mexico. *Archaeometry* 42(2): 301–316.

Baker, J., S. Stos, and T. Waight
2006 Lead Isotope Analysis of Archaeological Metals by Multiple-Collector Inductively Coupled Plasma Mass Spectrometry. *Archaeometry* 48(1): 45–56.

Baxter, M. J.
1994   *Exploratory Multivariate Analysis in Archaeology*. Edinburgh University Press, Edinburgh.

Bernardini, Wesley
1998   Conflict, Migration, and the Social Environment: Interpreting Change in Early and Late Pueblo IV Aggregations. In *Migration and Reorganization: The Pueblo IV Period in the American Southwest*, edited by Katherine A. Spielmann, pp. 91–114. *Arizona State University Anthropological Research Papers* 51. Arizona State University, Tempe.
2000   Kiln Firing Groups: Inter-Household Economic Collaboration and Social Organization in the Northern American Southwest. *American Antiquity* 65(2): 365–378.
2002   *The Gathering of the Clans: Understanding Ancestral Hopi Migration and Identity, A.D. 1275–1400*. Doctoral dissertation, Department of Anthropology, Arizona State University, Tempe. University Microfilms Inc., Ann Arbor.
2005   *Hopi Oral Tradition and the Archaeology of Identity*. University of Arizona Press, Tucson.

Bice, Richard A., Phyllis S. Davis, and William M. Sundt
2003   Indian Mining of Lead for Use in Rio Grande Glaze Paint, Report of the AS–5 Bethsheba Project Near Cerrillos, New Mexico. Albuquerque Archaeological Society, Albuquerque.

Bieberman, Robert A.
1951   Mineral Resources of the San Juan Basin. In *New Mexico Geological Society Guidebook of the South and West Sides of the San Juan Basin, 2nd Field Conference*, pp. 141–145. New Mexico Geological Society, Socorro.

Bishop, Ronald L., Robert L. Rands, and George R. Holley
1982   Ceramic Compositional Analysis in Archaeological Perspective. In *Advances in Archaeological Method and Theory*, Vol. 5, edited by Michael B. Schiffer, pp. 275–330. Academic Press, New York.

Bishop, Ronald L., Veletta Canouts, Suzanne P. De Atley, Alfred Quoyawayma, and C. W. Aikens
1988   The Formation of Ceramic Analytical Groups: Hopi Pottery Production and Exchange, A.D. 1300–1600. *Journal of Field Archaeology* 15: 317–337.

Blinman, Eric
1989   Potluck in the Protokiva: Ceramics and Ceremonialism in Pueblo I Villages. In "The Architecture of Social Integration in Prehistoric Pueblos," edited by William D. Lipe and Michelle Hegmon, pp. 113–134. *Crow Canyon Archaeological Center Occasional Paper* 1. Cortez.

Blinman, Eric, and Clint Swink
1997   Technology and Organization of Anasazi Trench Kilns. In "The Prehistory and History of Ceramic Kilns," edited by Prudence M. Rice, pp. 85–102. *Ceramics and Civilization*, Vol. 7. American Ceramic Society, Westerville, Ohio.

Bolviken, Erik, Ericka Helskog, Knut Helskog, Inger Marie Holm-Olsen, Leiv Solheim, and Reidar Bertelsen
1982   Correspondence Analysis: An Alternative to Principal Components. *World Archaeology* 14: 41–60.

Boni, M., G. Di Maio, R. Frei, and I. M. Villa
2000   Lead Isotopic Evidence for a Mixed Provenance for Roman Water Pipes from Pompeii. *Archaeometry* 42(1): 201–208.

Bower, Nathan W., Steve Faciszewski, Stephen Renwick, and Stewart Peckham
1986   A Preliminary Analysis of Rio Grande Glazes of the Classic Period Using Scanning Electron Microscopy with X-Ray Fluorescence. *Journal of Field Archaeology* 13: 307–315.

Brandt, Elizabeth A.
1980   On Secrecy and the Control of Knowledge. In *Secrecy: A Cross-Cultural Perspective*, edited by S. Tefft, pp. 123–146. Human Sciences Press, New York.

Braun, David P., and Stephen Plog
1982   Evolution of "Tribal" Social Networks: Theory and Prehistoric North American Evidence. *American Antiquity* 47(3): 504–525.

Brill, Robert H., and S. Moll
1963   The Electron-Beam Probe Microanalysis of Ancient Glass. In *Recent Advances in Conservation*, edited by Garry Thomson, pp. 145–151. Butterworths, London.

Brill, Robert H., and J. M. Wampler
1967   Isotope Studies of Ancient Lead. *American Journal of Archaeology* 71(1): 63–77.

Brill, Robert H., Kazuo Yamasaki, I. Lynus Barnes, K. J. R. Rossman, and Migdalia Diaz
1979   Lead Isotopes in Some Japanese and Chinese Glasses. *Ars Orientalis* 11: 87–109.

Brookins, D. G., and A. Majumdar
1982   The Sandia Granite: Single or Multiple Plutons? *New Mexico Geological Society Guidebook 22*, pp. 221–223. New Mexico Geological Society, Socorro.

Brunson, Judy L.
1985   Corrugated Ceramics as Indications of Interaction Spheres. In *Decoding Prehistoric Ceramics*, edited by Ben A. Nelson, pp. 102–127. Southern Illinois University Press, Carbondale and Edwardsville.

Bunzel, Ruth L.
1972   *The Pueblo Potter*. Dover Publications, New York.
1984   *Zuni Kachinas*. Rio Grande Press, Glorieta, New Mexico.
Burton, James H., and Arleyn W. Simon
1993   Acid Extraction as a Simple and Inexpensive Method for Compositional Characterization of Archaeological Ceramics. *American Antiquity* 58(1): 45–59.
Capone, Patricia
1997   Prehistoric Craft Specialization in Non-Hierarchical Societies: Petrographic Analysis of the Salinas Area, New Mexico, White Wares and Utility (Brown) Wares. Unpublished manuscript on file, Department of Anthropology, Arizona State University, Tempe.
2006   Rio Grande Glaze Ware Technology and Production: Historic Expediency. In *The Social Life of Pots: Glaze Wares and Cultural Dynamics in the Southwest, A.D. 1250–1680*, edited by Judith A. Habicht-Mauche, Suzanne L. Eckert, and Deborah L. Huntley, pp. 216–231. University of Arizona Press, Tucson.
Carlson, Roy L.
1970   White Mountain Redware: A Pottery Tradition of East-central Arizona and Western New Mexico. *Anthropological Papers of the University of Arizona* 19. University of Arizona Press, Tucson.
Carr, Christopher
1995   A Unified Middle-Range Theory of Artifact Design. In *Style, Society, and Person: Archaeological and Ethnological Perspectives*, edited by Christopher Carr and Jill E. Neitzel, pp. 171–258. Plenum Press, New York.
Chilton, Elizabeth S.
1998   The Cultural Origins of Technical Choice: Unraveling Algonquian and Iroquoian Ceramic Traditions in the Northeast. In *The Archaeology of Social Boundaries*, edited by Miriam T. Stark, pp. 132–160. Smithsonian Institution Press, Washington.
Clark, Tiffany C.
2006   Production, Exchange, and Social Identity: A Study of Chupadero Black-on-white Pottery. Doctoral dissertation, Department of Anthropology, Arizona State University, Tempe. University Microfilms, Inc., Ann Arbor.
Costin, Cathy L.
1991   Craft Specialization: Issues in Defining, Documenting, and Explaining the Organization of Production. In *Archaeological Method and Theory*, Vol. 3, edited by Michael B. Schiffer, pp. 1–56. University of Arizona Press, Tucson.

1998   Introduction: Craft and Social Identity. In "Craft and Social Identity," edited by Cathy L. Costin and Rita P. Wright, pp. 3–16. *Archaeological Papers of the American Anthropological Association* 8.
Crown, Patricia L.
1994   *Ceramics and Ideology: Salado Polychrome Pottery*. University of New Mexico Press, Albuquerque.
2000   Women's Role in Changing Cuisine. In *Women and Men in the Prehispanic Southwest: Labor, Power, and Prestige*, edited by Patricia L. Crown, pp. 221–266. School of American Research Press, Santa Fe.
Crown, Patricia L., and Ronald L. Bishop
1991   Manufacture of Gila Polychrome in the Greater American Southwest: An Instrumental Neutron Activation Analysis. In "Homol'ovi II: Archaeology of an Ancestral Hopi Village, Arizona," edited by E. Charles Adams and Kelley Ann Hays, pp. 49–56. *Anthropological Papers of the University of Arizona* 55. University of Arizona Press, Tucson.
Crown, Patricia L., and Wirt H. Wills
1995   The Origins of Southwestern Containers: Women's Time Allocation and Economic Intensification. *Journal of Anthropological Research* 51: 173–186.
Cumberpatch, C. G., and P. W. Blinkhorn, Editors
1997   Not So Much a Pot, More a Way of Life: Current Approaches to Artefact Analysis in Archaeology. *Oxbow Monograph* 83. Oxbow Books, Oxford.
Cushing, Frank H.
1894   Primitive Copper Working: An Experimental Study. *The American Anthropologist* 7: 93–117.
David, Nicholas, Judy Sterner, and Kodzo Gavua
1988   Why Pots Are Decorated. *Current Anthropology* 29(3): 365–389.
De Atley, Suzanne P.
1986   Mix and Match: Traditions of Glaze Paint Preparation at Four Mile Ruin, Arizona. In *Ceramics and Civilization*. Vol. II, *Technology and Style,* edited by William D. Kingery, pp. 1–56. The American Ceramic Society, Columbus, Ohio.
De Atley, Suzanne P., M. James Blackman, and Jacqueline S. Olin
1982   Comparison of Data Obtained by Neutron Activation and Electron Microprobe Analysis of Ceramics. In *Archaeological Ceramics*, edited by Jacqueline S. Olin and Alan D. Franklin, pp. 79–87. Smithsonian Institution Press, Washington.

DeBoer, Warren R.
1990   Interaction, Imitation, and Communication as Expressed in Style: The Ucayali Experience. In *The Uses of Style in Archaeology*, edited by Margaret Conkey and Christine Hastorf, pp. 82–104. Cambridge University Press, Cambridge.

Denio, Allen A.
1980   Chemistry for Potters. *Journal of Chemical Education* 57(4): 272–274.

Dietler, Michael, and Ingrid Herbich
1989   Tich Matek: The Technology of Luo Pottery Production and the Definition of Ceramic Style. *World Archaeology* 21(1): 148–164.
1998   Habitus, Techniques, Style: An Integrated Approach to the Social Understanding of Material Culture and Boundaries. In *The Archaeology of Social Boundaries*, edited by Miriam T. Stark, pp. 232–263. Smithsonian Institution Press, Washington.

Disbrow, Alan E., and Walter C. Stoll
1957   Geology of the Cerrillos Area, Santa Fe County, New Mexico. *State Bureau of Mines and Mineral Resources Bulletin* 48. New Mexico Institute of Mining and Technology, Socorro.

Dittert, Alfred E.
1959   Culture Change in the Cebolleta Mesa Region, Central Western New Mexico. Unpublished Ph.D. dissertation, Department of Anthropology, University of Arizona, Tucson.
1998   The Acoma Culture Province during the Period A.D. 1275–1500: Cultural Disruption and Reorganization. In "Migration and Reorganization: The Pueblo IV Period in the American Southwest," edited by Katherine A. Spielmann, pp. 81–89. *Arizona State University Anthropological Research Papers* 51. Tempe.

Duff, Andrew I.
1993   An Exploration of Post-Chacoan Community Organization through Ceramic Sourcing. MS, Master's thesis, Department of Anthropology, Arizona State University, Tempe.
1996   Ceramic Micro-Seriation: Types or Attributes? *American Antiquity* 61(1): 89–101.
1999   *Regional Interaction and the Transformation of Western Pueblo Identity, A.D. 1275–1400.* Doctoral dissertation, Department of Anthropology, Arizona State University, Tempe. University Microfilms, Inc., Ann Arbor.
2000   Scale, Interaction, and Regional Analysis in Late Pueblo Prehistory. In *The Archaeology of Regional Interaction: Religion, Warfare and Exchange Across the American Southwest and Beyond*, edited by Michelle Hegmon, pp. 71–98. University of Colorado Press, Boulder.
2002   *Western Pueblo Identities: Regional Interaction, Migration, and Transformation.* University of Arizona Press, Tucson.

Duff, Andrew I., and Keith W. Kintigh
1997   Beyond Microseriation: Chronology, Ceramics, and Social Process. Paper presented in the Symposium "Using Seriation in Processual Archaeology." 62nd Annual Meeting of the Society for American Archaeology, Nashville.

Dutton, Bertha
1963   *Sun Father's Way.* University of New Mexico Press, Albuquerque.

Eckert, Suzanne L.
1995   The Process of Aggregation in the Post-Chacoan Era: A Case Study from the Lower Zuni River Region. MS, Master's Thesis, Department of Anthropology, Arizona State University, Tempe.
2006   The Production and Distribution of Glaze-Painted Pottery in the Pueblo Southwest: A Synthesis. In *The Social Life of Pots: Glaze Wares and Cultural Dynamics in the Southwest, A.D. 1250–1680*, edited by Judith A. Habicht-Mauche, Suzanne L. Eckert, and Deborah L. Huntley, pp. 34–59. University of Arizona Press, Tucson.

Elston, Wolfgang E.
1961   Mineral Resources of Bernalillo, Sandoval, and Santa Fe Counties, New Mexico (Exclusive of Oil and Gas). In *New Mexico Geological Society Guidebook, 12th Field Conference*, edited by Stuart A. Northrop, pp. 155–167. New Mexico Geological Society, Socorro.

Ellis, F. Hawley
1981   Comments on Four Papers Pertaining to the Protohistoric Southwest. In "The Protohistoric Period in the North American Southwest, A.D. 1400–1700," edited by David R. Wilcox and W. Bruce Masse, pp. 410–413. *Arizona State University Anthropological Research Papers* 24. Tempe.

Eveleth, Robert
2002   Early Days at Hansonburg, New Mexico. Manuscript on file in New Mexico Bureau of Geology and Mineral Resources Archive, Socorro.

Ewing, Thomas E.
1979   Lead Isotope Data From Mineral Deposits of Southern New Mexico: A Reinterpretation. *Economic Geology* 74: 678–684.

Fenn, Thomas R., Barbara J. Mills, and Maren Hopkins
2006   The Social Contexts of Glaze Paint Ceramic Production and Consumption in the Silver Creek Area. In *The Social Life of Pots: Glaze*

Wares and Cultural Dynamics in the Southwest, A.D. 1250–1680, edited by Judith A. Habicht-Mauche, Suzanne L. Eckert, and Deborah L. Huntley, pp. 60–85. University of Arizona Press, Tucson.

Ferguson, T. J., and E. Richard Hart
1985   *A Zuni Atlas.* University of Oklahoma Press, Norman.

File, Lucien A.
1965   Directory of Mines of New Mexico. *New Mexico Bureau of Mines and Mineral Resources Circular 77.* New Mexico Bureau of Mines and Mineral Resources, Socorro.

Ford, Richard I.
1972   Barter, Gift, or Violence: An Analysis of Tewa Intertribal Exchange. In "Social Exchange and Interaction," edited by Edwin N. Wilmsen, pp. 21–45. *Museum of Anthropology Anthropological Papers* 46. University of Michigan, Ann Arbor.

Fowler, Andrew P., and John R. Stein
1992   The Anasazi Great House in Space, Time and Paradigm. In "Anasazi Regional Organization and the Chaco System," edited by David E. Doyel, pp. 101–122. *Maxwell Museum of Anthropology Anthropological Papers* 5. University of New Mexico, Albuquerque.

Fowler, Andrew P., John R. Stein, and Roger Anyon
1987   An Archaeological Reconnaissance of West-Central New Mexico, The Anasazi Monuments Project. Report submitted to State of New Mexico, Office of Cultural Affairs, Historic Preservation Division, Santa Fe.

Freestone, I. C.
1982   Application and Potential of Electron Probe Micro-Analysis in Technological and Provenance Investigations of Ancient Ceramics. *Archaeometry* 24(2): 99–116.

Gale, Noël H., and Zofia Stos-Gale
1982   Bronze Age Copper Sources in the Mediterranean: A New Approach. *Science* 216(4541): 11–18.
1993   Evaluating Lead Isotope Data: Further Observations: Comments…II. *Archaeometry* 35(2): 252–259.

Giles, D. L.
1991   Geologic Outline of the Cerrillos Mining District, Cerrillos Porphyry Copper Deposit, and Associated Mineralization. In "Field Guide to Geologic Excursions in New Mexico and Adjacent Areas of Texas and Colorado," edited by Betsy Julian and Jiri Zidek, pp. 62–65. *New Mexico Bureau of Mines and Mineral Resources Bulletin* 137. New Mexico Bureau of Mines and Mineral Resources, Socorro.

Glascock, Michael D.
1992   Characterization of Archaeological Ceramics at MURR by Neutron Activational Analysis and Multivariate Statistics. In "Chemical Characterization of Ceramic Pastes in Archaeology," edited by Hector Neff, pp. 11–26. *Monographs in World Archaeology* 7. Prehistory Press, Madison, Wisconsin.

Glowacki, Donna M., and Hector Neff, Editors
2002   Ceramic Production and Circulation in the Greater Southwest: Source Determination by INAA and Complementary Mineralogical Investigations. *Cotsen Institute Monograph* 44. The Cotsen Institute of Archaeology, University of California, Los Angeles.

Goffer, Zvi
1980   *Archaeological Chemistry: A Sourcebook on the Applications of Chemistry to Archaeology.* John Wiley and Sons, New York.

Goldfrank, Esther S.
1970   *Isleta Paintings.* With an introduction by Elsie Clews Parsons. Smithsonian Institution Press, Washington.

Gosselain, Olivier P.
1998   Social and Technical Identity in a Clay Crystal Ball. In *The Archaeology of Social Boundaries*, edited by Miriam T. Stark, pp. 78–106. Smithsonian Institution Press, Washington.
2000   Materializing Identities: An African Perspective. *Journal of Archaeological Method and Theory* 7: 187–217.

Graves, Michael W.
1991   Pottery Production and Distribution among the Kalinga: A Study of Household and Regional Organization and Differentiation. In *Ceramic Ethnoarchaeology*, edited by William A. Longacre, pp. 112–143. University of Arizona Press, Tucson.
1994   Community Boundaries in Late Prehistoric Puebloan Society: Kalinga Ethnoarchaeology as a Model for the Production and Exchange of Pottery. In *The Ancient Southwestern Community*, edited by Wirt H. Wills and Robert D. Leonard, pp. 149–169. University of New Mexico Press, Albuquerque.

Graves, William M.
1996   Social Power and Prestige Enhancement Among the Protohistoric Salinas Pueblos, Rio Grande Valley, New Mexico. MS, Master's Thesis, Department of Anthropology, Arizona State University, Tempe.
2002   *Power, Autonomy, and Inequality in Rio Grande Puebloan Society, A.D. 1300–1672.* Doctoral dissertation, Arizona State University, Tempe. University Microfilms, Inc., Ann Arbor.

Graves, William M. (*continued*)
2004   Social Identity and the Internal Organization of the Jumanos Pueblos Settlement Cluster in the Salinas District, Central New Mexico. In *The Protohistoric Pueblo World, A.D. 1275–1600*, edited by E. Charles Adams and Andrew I. Duff, pp. 43–52. University of Arizona Press, Tucson.

Graves, William M., and Suzanne Eckert
1998   Decorated Ceramic Distributions and Ideological Developments in the Northern and Central Rio Grande Valley, New Mexico. In "Migration and Reorganization: The Pueblo IV Period in the American Southwest," edited by Katherine A Spielmann, pp. 263–283. *Arizona State University Anthropological Research Papers* 51. Arizona State University, Tempe.

Graves, William M., and Katherine A. Spielmann
2000   Leadership, Long-Distance Exchange, and Feasting in the Protohistoric Rio Grande. In *Alternative Leadership Strategies in the Prehispanic Southwest*, edited by Barbara J. Mills, pp. 45–59. University of Arizona Press, Tucson.

Green, David
1973   *Pottery Glazes*. Watson-Guptill Publications, New York.

Gulson, Brian L.
1986   *Lead Isotopes in Mineral Exploration*. Elsevier, Amsterdam.

Habicht-Mauche, Judith A.
1993   The Pottery from Arroyo Hondo Pueblo, New Mexico: Tribalization and Trade in the Northern Rio Grande. *Arroyo Hondo Archaeological Series,* Vol. 8. School of American Research Press, Santa Fe.
1995   Changing Patterns of Pottery Manufacture and Trade in the Northern Rio Grande Region. In *Ceramic Production in the American Southwest*, edited by Barbara J. Mills and Patricia L. Crown, pp. 167–199. University of Arizona Press, Tucson.

Habicht-Mauche, Judith A., Stephen T. Glenn, Homer Milford, and A. Russell Flegal
2000   Isotopic Tracing of Prehistoric Rio Grande Glaze-Paint Production and Trade. *Journal of Archaeological Science* 27: 709–713.

Habicht-Mauche, Judith A., Stephen T. Glenn, Mike P. Schmidt, Rob Franks, Homer Milford, and A. Russell Flegal
2002   Stable Lead Isotope Analysis of Rio Grande Glaze Paints and Ores Using ICP-MS: A Comparison of Acid Dissolution and Laser Ablation Techniques. *Journal of Archaeological Science* 29: 1043–1053.

Hagstrum, Melissa B.
1995   Creativity and Craft: Household Pottery Traditions in the Southwest. In *Ceramic Production in the American Southwest*, edited by Barbara J. Mills and Patricia L. Crown, pp. 281–299. University of Arizona Press, Tucson.

Hammond, George P., and Agapito Rey
1966   The Rediscovery of New Mexico, 1580–1594: The Explorations of Chamuscado, Espejo, Castaño de Sosa, Morlete, and Leyva de Bonilla and Humaña. *Coronado Cuarto Centennial Publications, 1540–1940*, Vol. III. University of New Mexico Press, Albuquerque.

Hart, E. Richard
1984   Zuni Mining. Paper presented at the Annual Conference of the American Society for Ethnohistory, New Orleans.
1995   [Editor] Zuni and the Courts CD Rom, Produced by the Institute of the North American West. In *Zuni and the Courts: A Struggle for Sovereign Land Rights*, by E. Richard Hart. University of Kansas Press, Lawrence.

Hawley, Florence M.
1929   Prehistoric Pottery Pigments in the Southwest. *American Anthropologist* N.S.(31): 731–754.

Hawley, Fred G.
1938   The Chemical Analysis of Prehistoric Southwestern Glaze-Paint, with Components. *University of New Mexico Bulletin, Anthropological Series* 2(4): 15–27.

Hayden, Brian
1995   Pathways to Power: Principles for Creating Socioeconomic Inequalities. In *Foundations of Social Inequality*, edited by Steadman Upham, pp. 147–177. Cambridge University Press, Cambridge.

Hays-Gilpin, Kelley
2000   Gender Ideology and Ritual Activities. In *Women and Men in the Prehispanic Southwest: Labor, Power, and Prestige*, edited by Patricia L. Crown, pp. 91–135. School of American Research Press, Santa Fe.

Heck, M., and P. Hoffmann
2000   Coloured Opaque Glass Beads of the Merovingians. *Archaeometry* 42(2): 341–357.

Hegmon, Michelle
1998   Technology, Style, and Social Practices: Archaeological Approaches. In *The Archaeology of Social Boundaries*, edited by Miriam T. Stark, pp. 264–280. Smithsonian Institution Press, Washington.
2000   [Editor] *The Archaeology of Regional Interaction: Religion, Warfare and Exchange Across the American Southwest and Beyond*. University of Colorado Press, Boulder.

Helms, Mary W.
1993   *Craft and the Kingly Ideal: Art, Trade, and Power.* University of Texas Press, Austin.

Herhahn, Cynthia L.
1995   An Exploration of Technology Transfer in the Fourteenth Century Rio Grande Valley, New Mexico: A Compositional Analysis of Glaze Paints. MS, Master's Thesis, Department of Anthropology, Arizona State University, Tempe.
2006   Inferring Social Interactions from Pottery Recipes: Rio Grande Glaze Paint Composition and Cultural Transmission. In *The Social Life of Pots: Glaze Wares and Cultural Dynamics in the Southwest, A.D. 1250–1680*, edited by Judith A. Habicht-Mauche, Suzanne L. Eckert, and Deborah L. Huntley, pp. 179–196. University of Arizona Press, Tucson.

Herhahn, Cynthia L., and Eric Blinman
1999   Materials Science Meets the Artisan: A Look at Innovation through Experiments with Lead-glazed Paints from the American Southwest. Paper presented at the 64th Annual Meeting of the Society for American Archaeology, March 24–28, Chicago.

Hibben, Frank C.
1975   *Kiva Art of the Anasazi at Pottery Mound.* K. C. Publications, Las Vegas.

Hill, Jane H.
2001   The Zuni Language in Southwestern Areal Context. Paper presented at the Zuñi-Mogollon Seminar, Museum of Northern Arizona, October 14–19.

Huntley, Deborah L.
1997   Glaze Paint Technology in the Late Prehistoric Zuni Region: A Chemical Compositional Analysis. Paper presented at the 62nd Annual Meeting of the Society for American Archaeology, Nashville.
2004   *Interaction, Boundaries and Identities: A Multiscalar Approach to the Organizational Scale of Pueblo IV Zuni Society.* Doctoral Dissertation, Department of Anthropology, Arizona State University, Tempe. University Microfilms, Inc., Ann Arbor.
2006   From Recipe to Identity: Exploring Zuni Glaze Ware Communities of Practice. In *The Social Life of Pots: Glaze Wares and Cultural Dynamics in the Southwest, A.D. 1250–1680*, edited by Judith A. Habicht-Mauche, Suzanne L. Eckert, and Deborah L. Huntley, pp. 105–123. University of Arizona Press, Tucson.

Huntley, Deborah L., and Cynthia L. Herhahn
1996   Technological Change and the Development of Rio Grande Craft Specialization. Paper presented at the 1996 Chacmool Conference, Calgary.

Huntley, Deborah L., and Keith W. Kintigh
2004   Archaeological Patterning and Organizational Scale of Late Prehistoric Settlement Clusters in the Zuni Region of New Mexico. In *The Protohistoric Pueblo World, A.D. 1275–1600*, edited by E. Charles Adams and Andrew I. Duff, pp. 62–74. University of Arizona Press, Tucson.

Huntley, Deborah L., and Gregson Schachner
1999   The Los Gigantes Community: Post-Chacoan Settlement in the Zuni Region of the American Southwest. Poster presented at the 64th Annual Meeting of the Society for American Archaeology, Chicago.

Huntley, Deborah L., Katherine A. Spielmann, Judith A. Habicht-Mauche, Cynthia L. Herhahn, and A. Russell Flegal
2007   Local Recipes or Distant Commodities? Lead Isotope and Chemical Compositional Analysis of Glaze Paints from the Salinas Pueblos, New Mexico. *Journal of Archaeological Science* 34(7): 1135–1147.

Jones, Deborah L.
1995   Identifying Production Groups Within a Single Community: Rio Grande Glaze-Decorated Ceramics at Quarai Pueblo. MS, Masters Thesis, Department of Anthropology, Arizona State University, Tempe.

Kidder, Alfred V.
1924   An Introduction to Southwestern Archaeology with a Preliminary Account of the Excavations at Pecos. *Papers of the Southwestern Expedition* 1. Published for the Phillips Academy by Yale University Press, New Haven.

Kintigh, Keith W.
1985a   Settlement, Subsistence, and Society in Late Zuni Prehistory. *Anthropological Papers of the University of Arizona* 44. University of Arizona Press, Tucson.
1985b   Social Structure, the Structure of Style, and Stylistic Pattern in Cibola Pottery. In *Decoding Prehistoric Ceramics*, edited by Ben A. Nelson, pp. 35–74. Southern Illinois University Press, Carbondale and Edwardsville.
1990   Protohistoric Transitions in the Western Pueblo Area. In *Perspectives on Southwestern Prehistory*, edited by Paul E. Minnis and Charles L. Redman, pp. 258–275. Westview Press, Boulder, Colorado.
1994   Chaco, Community Architecture, and Cibolan Aggregation. In *The Ancient Southwestern Community: Models and Methods for the Study of Prehistoric Social Organization*, edited by

Kintigh, Keith W. (*continued*)
Wirt H. Wills and Robert D. Leonard, pp. 131–140. University of New Mexico Press, Albuquerque.

1996   The Cibola Region in the Post-Chacoan Era. In *The Prehistoric Pueblo World: A.D. 1150–1350*, edited by Michael A. Adler, pp. 131–144. University of Arizona Press, Tucson.

1997   Report on Mapping the Box S Site. Manuscript on file, Department of Anthropology, Arizona State University, Tempe.

2000   Leadership Strategies in Protohistoric Zuni Towns. In *Alternative Leadership Strategies in the Prehispanic Southwest*, edited by Barbara J. Mills, pp. 95–116. University of Arizona Press, Tucson.

2002   *Tools for Quantitative Archaeology: Programs for Quantitative Analysis in Archaeology*. Manual accompanying computer programs. Department of Anthropology, Arizona State University, Tempe.

2007   Late Prehistoric and Protohistoric Settlement Systems in the Zuni Area. In *Zuni Origins: Toward a New Synthesis of Southwestern Archaeology*, edited by David A. Gregory and David R. Wilcox, pp. 361–376. University of Arizona Press, Tucson.

Kintigh, Keith W., and A. Ammerman
1982   Heuristic Approaches to Spatial Analysis in Archaeology. *American Antiquity* 47(1): 31–63.

Kintigh, Keith W., Donna M. Glowacki, and Deborah L. Huntley
2004   Long-term Settlement History and the Emergence of Towns in the Zuni Area. *American Antiquity* 69(3): 432–456.

Kintigh, Keith W., Todd L. Howell, and Andrew I. Duff
1996   Post-Chacoan Social Integration at the Hinkson Site, New Mexico. *The Kiva* 61(3): 257–274.

Lave, Jean, and Etienne Wenger
1991   *Situated Learning: Legitimate Peripheral Participation*. Cambridge University Press, Cambridge.

LeBlanc, Steven A.
1975   Micro-Seriation: A Method for Fine Chronologic Differentiation. *American Antiquity* 40(1): 22–38.

1976   Temporal and Ceramic Relationships between Some Late PIII Sites in the Zuni Area. *Plateau* 48(3 and 4): 75–83.

1978   Settlement Patterns in the El Morro Valley, New Mexico. In *Investigations of the Southwestern Anthropological Research Group*, edited by Robert Euler and George Gumerman, pp. 45–51. Museum of Northern Arizona, Flagstaff.

1989   Cibola: Shifting Cultural Boundaries. In *Dynamics of Southwest Prehistory*, edited by Linda S. Cordell and George J. Gumerman, pp. 337–369. Smithsonian Institution Press, Washington.

1998   Settlement Consequences of Warfare During the Late Pueblo III and Pueblo IV Periods. In "Migration and Reorganization: The Pueblo IV Period in the American Southwest," edited by Katherine A. Spielmann, pp. 115–135. *Arizona State University Anthropological Research Papers* 51. Arizona State University, Tempe.

1999   *Prehistoric Warfare in the American Southwest*. University of Utah Press, Salt Lake City.

2000   Regional Interaction and Warfare in the Late Prehistoric Southwest. In *The Archaeology of Regional Interaction: Religion, Warfare and Exchange Across the American Southwest and Beyond*, edited by Michelle Hegmon, pp. 41–70. University of Colorado Press, Boulder.

2001   Warfare and Aggregation in the El Morro Valley, New Mexico. In *Deadly Landscapes: Case Studies in Prehistoric Southwestern Warfare*, edited by Glen E. Rice and Steven A. LeBlanc, pp. 19–49. University of Utah Press, Salt Lake City.

Lekson, Stephen H., Curtis P. Nepstad-Thornberry, Brian E. Yunker, Toni S. Laumbach, David P. Cain, and Karl W. Laumbach
2002   Migrations in the Southwest: Pinnacle Ruin, Southwestern New Mexico. *Kiva* 68(2): 73–101.

Lemonnier, Pierre
1992   Elements for an Anthropology of Technology. *University of Michigan Anthropological Papers* 88. Museum of Anthropology, University of Michigan, Ann Arbor.

1993   Introduction. In *Technological Choices: Transformation in Material Cultures Since the Neolithic*, edited by Pierre Lemonnier, pp. 1–35. Routledge, London.

Levy, Jerrold E.
1994   Ethnographic Analogs: Strategies for Reconstructing Archaeological Cultures. In "Understanding Complexity in the Prehistoric Southwest," edited by George J. Gumerman and Murray Gell-Mann, pp. 223–244. *Santa Fe Institute Studies in the Sciences of Complexity, Proceedings*, Vol. 16. Addison-Wesley, Reading.

Lightfoot, Kent G., and Steadman Upham
1989   Complex Societies in the Prehistoric American Southwest: A Consideration of the Controversy. In *The Sociopolitical Structure of Prehistoric Southwestern Societies*, edited by

Steadman Upham, Kent G. Lightfoot, and Roberta A. Jewett, pp. 389–418. Westview Press, Boulder.

Lindgren, W., Louis C. Graton, and C. H. Gordon
1910 The Ore Deposits of New Mexico. *USGS Professional Paper 68.* Washington.

MacEachern, Scott
1998 Scale, Style and Cultural Variation: Technological Traditions in the Northern Mandara Mountains. In *The Archaeology of Social Boundaries*, edited by Miriam T. Stark, pp. 107–131. Smithsonian Institution Press, Washington.

Marquardt, William H.
1974 A Temporal Perspective on Late Prehistoric Societies in the Eastern Cibola Area. MS, Doctoral dissertation, Washington University, St. Louis.

Marshall, Michael P., and Henry J. Walt
1984 *The Rio Abajo: Prehistory and History of a Rio Grande Province.* New Mexico Historic Preservation Division, Santa Fe.

Matson, Frederick R.
1985 Glazed Brick from Babylon: Historical Setting and Microprobe Analysis. In *Ceramics and Civilization.* Vol. 3: *Technology and Style*, edited by William D. Kingery, pp.113–156. The American Ceramic Society, Columbus, Ohio.

Maxwell, C. H., and L. G. Nonini
1977 Status of Mineral Resource Information for the Zuni Indian Reservation, New Mexico. *Bureau of Indian Affairs Administrative Report 37*, pp. 25–28.

McGuire, Randall H., and Dean J. Saitta
1996 Although They Have Petty Captains, They Obey Them Badly: The Dialectics of Prehispanic Western Pueblo Social Organization. *American Antiquity* 61(2): 197–216.

Mills, Barbara J.
1995 The Organization of Protohistoric Zuni Ceramic Production. In *Ceramic Production in the American Southwest*, edited by Barbara J. Mills and Patricia L. Crown, pp. 200–230. University of Arizona Press, Tucson.
1999a Ceramic Ware and Type Systematics. In "Living on the Edge of the Rim: Excavations and Analysis of the Silver Creek Archaeological Research Project, 1993–1998," edited by Barbara J. Mills, Sarah A. Herr, and Scott Van Keuren, pp. 243–268. *Arizona State Museum Archaeological Series* 192. University of Arizona, Tucson.
1999b Ceramics and Social Contexts of Food Production in the Northern Southwest. In *Pottery and People: A Dynamic Interaction*, edited by

James M. Skibo and Gary M. Feinman, pp. 99–114. University of Utah Press, Salt Lake City.
2000 Gender, Craft Production, and Inequality. In *Women and Men in the Prehispanic Southwest: Labor, Power, and Prestige*, edited by Patricia L. Crown, pp. 301–343. School of American Research Press, Santa Fe.
2007 A Regional Perspective on Ceramics and Zuni Identity, AD 200–1630. In *Zuni Origins: Toward a New Synthesis of Southwestern Archaeology*, edited by David A. Gregory and David R. Wilcox, pp. 210–238. University of Arizona Press, Tucson.

Mills, Barbara J., and Patricia L. Crown, Editors
1995 *Ceramic Production in the American Southwest.* University of Arizona Press, Tucson.

Mills, Barbara J., and Sarah A. Herr
1999 Chronology of the Mogollon Rim Region. In "Living on the Edge of the Rim: Excavations and Analysis of the Silver Creek Archaeological Research Project, 1993–1998," edited by Barbara J. Mills, Sarah A. Herr, and Scott Van Keuren, pp. 269–293. *Arizona State Museum Archaeological Series* 192. University of Arizona, Tucson.

Mills, Barbara J., Sarah A. Herr, Susan L. Stinson, and Daniela Triadan
1999 Ceramic Production and Distribution. In "Living on the Edge of the Rim: Excavations and Analysis of the Silver Creek Archaeological Research Project, 1993–1998," edited by Barbara J. Mills, Sarah A. Herr and Scott Van Keuren, pp. 295–324. *Arizona State Museum Archaeological Series* 192. University of Arizona, Tucson.

Minar, C. Jill
2001 Motor Skills and the Learning Process: The Conservation of Cordage Final Twist Direction in Communities of Practice. *Journal of Anthropological Research* 57: 381–405.

Mindeleff, Victor
1891 *A Study of Pueblo Architecture: Tusayan and Cibola.* Reprinted 1989. Smithsonian Institution Press, Washington.

Mobley-Tanaka, Jeannette
1998 An Analysis of Design on Glaze Ware Sherds from the Salinas Area, New Mexico. Manuscript on file, Department of Anthropology, Arizona State University, Tempe.

Neff, Hector
2002a Quantitative Techniques for Analyzing Ceramic Compositional Data. In "Ceramic Production and Circulation in the Greater South

Neff, Hector (*continued*)
west: Source Determination by INAA and Complementary Mineralogical Investigations," edited by Donna M. Glowacki and Hector Neff, pp. 15–36. *Cotsen Institute Monograph* 44. The Cotsen Institute of Archaeology, University of California, Los Angeles.

2002b Unpublished letter prepared at the University of Missouri Research Reactor Center, Columbia.

Neff, Hector, and Donna M. Glowacki
2002 Ceramic Source Determination by Instrumental Neutron Activation Analysis in the American Southwest. In "Ceramic Production and Circulation in the Greater Southwest: Source Determination by INAA and Complementary Mineralogical Investigations," edited by Donna M. Glowacki and Hector Neff, pp. 1–14. *Cotsen Institute Monograph* 44. The Cotsen Institute of Archaeology, University of California, Los Angeles.

Neitzel, Jill E.
2000 What Is a Regional System? Issues of Scale and Interaction in the Prehistoric Southwest. In *The Archaeology of Regional Interaction: Religion, Warfare and Exchange Across the American Southwest and Beyond*, edited by Michelle Hegmon, pp. 25–40. University of Colorado Press, Boulder.

1999 [Editor] *Great Towns and Regional Polities in the Prehistoric American Southwest and Southeast*. University of New Mexico Press, Albuquerque.

Nelson, Kit, and Judith A. Habicht-Mauche
2006 Lead, Paint, and Pots: Rio Grande Intercommunity Dynamics from a Glaze Ware Perspective. In *The Social Life of Pots: Glaze Wares and Cultural Dynamics in the Southwest, A.D. 1250–1680*, edited by Judith A. Habicht-Mauche, Suzanne L. Eckert, and Deborah L. Huntley, pp. 197–215. University of Arizona Press, Tucson.

New Mexico Geological Society
1996 *New Mexico Highway Geologic Map*. New Mexico Geological Society in cooperation with New Mexico Bureau of Mines and Mineral Resources. 1:1,000,000. Albuquerque.

Northrop, Stuart A.
1996 *Minerals of New Mexico* (Third Edition). University of New Mexico Press, Albuquerque.

Plog, Fred
1985 Status and Death at Grasshopper Pueblo: The Homogenization of Reality. In "Status, Structure, and Stratification: Current Archaeological Reconstruction." *Proceedings of the 16th Chacmool Conference*, edited by M. Thompson, M. T. Garcia, and F. J. Kense, pp. 161–165. University of Calgary, Canada.

Plog, Fred, and Steadman Upham
1983 The Analysis of Prehistoric Political Organization. In *Development of Political Organization in Native North America*, edited by E. Tooker and M. Fried, pp. 199–213. American Ethnological Society, Washington.

Plog, Stephen
1980 *Stylistic Variation in Prehistoric Ceramics: Design Analysis in the American Southwest*. Cambridge University Press, Cambridge.

Plog, Stephen, and Julie Solometo
1997 The Never-Changing and the Ever-Changing: The Evolution of Western Pueblo Ritual. *Cambridge Archaeological Journal* 7(2): 161–182.

Potter, James M.
1997 Communal Ritual, Feasting, and Social Differentiation in Late Prehistoric Zuni Communities. Doctoral dissertation, Arizona State University, Tempe. University Microfilms, Inc., Ann Arbor.

1998 The Structure of Open Space in Late Prehistoric Settlements in the Southwest. In "Migration and Reorganization: The Pueblo IV Period in the American Southwest," edited by Katherine A. Spielmann, pp. 137–164. *Arizona State University Anthropological Research Papers* 51, Tempe.

Potter, James M., and Elizabeth M. Perry
2000 Ritual as a Power Resource in the American Southwest. In *Alternative Leadership Strategies in the Prehispanic Southwest*, edited by Barbara J. Mills, pp. 60–78. University of Arizona Press, Tucson.

Rappaport, Roy
1968 *Pigs for the Ancestors: Ritual and Ecology of a New Guinea People*. Yale University Press, New Haven.

1979 Ritual Regulation of Environmental Relations among a New Guinea People. In *Ecology, Meaning, and Religion*, edited by Roy Rappaport, pp. 27–42. North Atlantic Books, Richmond, California.

Reed, S. J. B.
1993 *Electron Microprobe Analysis*. Cambridge University Press, Cambridge.

Reid, J. Jefferson, and Stephanie M. Whittlesey
1999 *Grasshopper Pueblo: A Study of Archaeology and Ancient Life*. University of Arizona Press, Tucson.

Rhodes, Daniel
1973 *Clay and Glazes for the Potter*. Chilton Book Company, Radnor, Pennsylvania.

Rice, Prudence M.
1987 *Pottery Analysis: A Sourcebook.* University of Chicago Press, Chicago.

Riley, Carroll L.
1975 The Road to Hawikuh: Trade and Trade Routes to Cibola-Zuni During the Late Prehistoric and Early Historic Times. *The Kiva* 41(2): 137–159.

Riley, Carroll L., and J. L. Manson
1983 The Cibola-Tiguex Route: Continuity and Change in the Southwest. *The New Mexico Historical Review* 58(4): 350–363.

Rothschild, Nan A., and Susan A. Dublin
1995 The Zuni Farming Village Study and Excavations at Lower Pescado Village: A Report on the Columbia/Barnard Archaeological Field School, 1989–1991. Unpublished manuscript in the authors' possession.

Rye, Owen S., and Clifford Evans
1976 Traditional Pottery Techniques of Pakistan. *Smithsonian Contributions to Anthropology* 21. Smithsonian Institution Press, Washington.

Sackett, James R.
1977 The Meaning of Style in Archaeology: A General Model. *American Antiquity* 43(3): 369–380.
1990 Style and Ethnicity in Archaeology: The Case for Isochrestism. In *The Uses of Style in Archaeology*, edited by Margaret W. Conkey and Christine A. Hastorf, pp. 32–43. Cambridge University Press, Cambridge.

Sahlins, Marshall D.
1972 *Stone Age Economics.* Aldine, Chicago.

Sassaman, Kenneth E., and Wicktoria Rudolphi
2001 Communities of Practice in the Early Pottery Traditions of the American Southwest. *Journal of Anthropological Research* 57: 407–425.

Sayre, E. V., K. A. Yener, E. C. Joel, and I. L. Barnes
1992 Statistical Evaluation of the Presently Accumulated Lead Isotope Data from Anatolia and Surrounding Regions. *Archaeometry* 34(1): 73–105.

Schachner, Gregson
2006 The Decline of Zuni Glaze Ware Production in the Tumultuous Fifteenth Century. In *The Social Life of Pots: Glaze Wares and Cultural Dynamics in the Southwest, A.D. 1250–1680*, edited by Judith A. Habicht-Mauche, Suzanne L. Eckert, and Deborah L. Huntley, pp. 124–141. University of Arizona Press, Tucson.
2007 *Population Circulation and the Transformation of Ancient Cibola Communities.* Doctoral dissertation, Arizona State University, Tempe. University Microfilms, Inc., Ann Arbor.

Schroeder, Albert H.
1979 The Cerrillos Mining Area. In "Archaeology and History of Santa Fe County," edited by Raymond V. Ingersoll, pp. 13–16. *New Mexico Geological Society Special Publication* 8. Albuquerque.

Seventh Southwestern Ceramic Seminar
1965 *Acoma-Zuni Pottery Types.* Research Center, Museum of Northern Arizona. Flagstaff, Arizona. September 24–25.

Shepard, Anna O.
1942 Rio Grande Glaze Paint Ware, A Study Illustrating the place of Ceramic Technological Analysis in Archaeological Research. *Carnegie Institution of Washington, Publication* 528, *Contribution* 39. Washington.
1956 *Ceramics for the Archaeologist.* Carnegie Institution of Washington, Washington.
1965 Rio Grande Glaze Paint Pottery: A Test of Petrographic Analysis. In *Ceramics and Man*, edited by Frederick R. Matson, pp. 62–87. Aldine, Chicago.

Simon, Arleyn W., James H. Burton, and David R. Abbott
1998 Intraregional Connections in the Development and Distribution of Salado Polychromes in Central Arizona. *Journal of Anthropological Research* 54: 519–547.

Slawson, William F., and Carl F. Austin
1960 Anomalous Leads from a Selected Geological Environment in West-Central New Mexico. *Nature* 187(4735): 400–401.

Smith, Watson
1952 Kiva Mural Decorations at Awatovi and Kawaika-a, with a Survey of Other Wall Paintings in the Pueblo Southwest. *Papers of the Peabody Museum of American Archaeology and Ethnology* 37. Harvard University, Cambridge.

Snow, David H.
1981 Protohistoric Rio Grande Pueblo Economies: A Review of Trends. In "The Protohistoric Period in the Southwest: 1450–1700," edited by David R. Wilcox and W. Bruce Masse, pp. 354–376. *Arizona State University Anthropological Research Papers* 24. Arizona State University, Tempe.
1982 The Rio Grande Glaze, Matte-Paint, and Plainware Tradition. In "Southwestern Ceramics: A Comparative Review," edited by Albert H. Schroeder, pp. 235–278. *Arizona Archaeologist* 15. Arizona Archaeological Society, Phoenix.

South, Stanley
1978 Research Strategies for Archaeological Pattern Recognition on Historic Sites. *World Archaeology* 10: 36–50.

Spielmann, Katherine A.

1989   Colonists, Hunters, and Farmers: Plains-Pueblo Interaction in the 17th Century. In *Columbian Consequences*, Vol. 1., edited by David Hurst Thomas, pp. 101–113. Smithsonian Institution Press, Washington.

1994   Clustered Confederacies: Sociopolitical Organization in the Protohistoric Rio Grande. In *The Ancient Southwestern Community*, edited by Wirt H. Wills and Robert D. Leonard, pp. 45–54. University of New Mexico Press, Albuquerque.

1998   Ritual Influences on the Development of Rio Grande Glaze A Ceramics. In "Migration and Reorganization: The Pueblo IV Period in the American Southwest," edited by Katherine A. Spielmann, pp. 253–261. *Arizona State University Anthropological Research Papers* 51. Arizona State University, Tempe.

2000   Gender and Exchange. In *Women and Men in the Prehispanic Southwest: Labor, Power, and Prestige*, edited by Patricia L. Crown, pp. 345–377. School of American Research Press, Santa Fe.

Spier, Leslie

1917   An Outline for a Chronology of Zuni Ruins. *Anthropological Papers of the American Museum of Natural History* 18(3).

Stanislawski, Michael B.

1978   If Pots Were Mortal. In *Explorations in Ethnoarchaeology*, edited by Richard A. Gould, pp. 201–228. University of New Mexico Press, Albuquerque.

Stark, Miriam T.

1992   From Sibling to Suki: Social Relations and Spatial Proximity in Kalinga Pottery Exchange. *Journal of Anthropological Archaeology* 11: 137–151.

1998a   Technical Choices and Social Boundaries in Material Culture Patterning: An Introduction. In *The Archaeology of Social Boundaries*, edited by Miriam T. Stark, pp. 1–11. Smithsonian Institution Press, Washington.

1998b   [Editor] *The Archaeology of Social Boundaries*. Smithsonian Institution Press, Washington.

Stark, Miriam T., Mark D. Elson, and Jeffery J. Clark

1998   Social Boundaries and Technical Choices in Tonto Basin Prehistory. In *The Archaeology of Social Boundaries*, edited by Miriam T. Stark, pp. 208–231. Smithsonian Institution Press, Washington.

Steinberg, Arthur, and Diana C. Kamilli

1984   Paint and Paste Studies of Selected Halaf Sherds From Mesopotamia. In "Pots and Potters: Current Approaches in Ceramic Archaeology," edited by Prudence M Rice, pp. 187–208. *Monograph* 24. Institute of Archaeology, University of California, Los Angeles.

Stevenson, Matilda Coxe

1904   The Zuni Indians: Their Mythology, Esoteric Fraternities, and Ceremonies. In *Twenty-third Annual Report of the Bureau of American Ethnology, 1901-1902*, pp. 3–364. Washington.

Stone, Tammy T.

1992   *The Process of Aggregation in the American Southwest: A Case Study from Zuni, New Mexico*. Doctoral dissertation, Department of Anthropology, Arizona State University, Tempe. University Microfilms, Inc., Ann Arbor.

1994   The Process of Aggregation in the Zuni Region: Reasons and Implications. In "Exploring Social, Political and Economic Organization in the Zuni Region," edited by Todd L. Howell and Tammy Stone, pp. 9–23. *Arizona State University Anthropological Research Papers* 46. Arizona State University, Tempe.

1999   The Chaos of Collapse: Disintegration and Reintegration of Inter-regional Systems. *Antiquity* 73: 110–118.

Stos-Gale, Zofia A.

1992   Isotope Archaeology: Reading the Past in Metals, Minerals, and Bone. *Endeavor, New Series* 16(2): 85–90.

Strazicich, Nicola M.

1995   *Prehistoric Pottery Production in the Chalchihuites and La Quemada Regions of Zacatecas, Mexico*. Doctoral dissertation, Department of Anthropology, SUNY Buffalo. University Microfilms, Inc., Ann Arbor.

Thomas, David Hurst

1986   *Refiguring Anthropology: First Principles of Probability and Statistics*. Waveland Press, Prospect Heights, Illinois.

Triadan, Daniela

1997   Ceramic Commodities and Common Containers: Production and Distribution of White Mountain Red Ware in the Grasshopper Region, Arizona. *Anthropological Papers of the University of Arizona* 61. University of Arizona Press, Tucson.

United States Geological Survey

1969   Mineral and Water Resources of Arizona. *Arizona Bureau of Mines Bulletin 180*. University of Arizona, Tucson.

1982   Mineral and Water Resources of New Mexico. *New Mexico Bureau of Mines and Mineral Resources Bulletin 87* (reprint). New Mexico Bureau of Mines and Mineral Resources, Socorro.

Upham, Steadman
1982 *Polities and Power: An Economic and Political History of the Western Pueblo.* Academic Press, New York.

Upham, Steadman, and Fred Plog
1986 The Interpretation of Prehistoric Political Complexity in the Central and Northern Southwest: Toward a Mending of the Models. *Journal of Field Archaeology* 12: 223–238.

Upham, Steadman, and Lori S. Reed
1989 Regional Systems in the Central and Northern Southwest: Demography, Economy, and Sociopolitics Preceding Contact. In *Columbian Consequences*, Vol. 1, edited by David Hurst Thomas, pp. 57–76. Smithsonian Institution Press, Washington.

Van Keuren, Scott, Susan L. Stinson, and David R. Abbott
1997 Specialized Production of Hohokam Plain Ware Ceramics in the Lower Salt River Valley. *Kiva* 63(2): 155–175.

Warren, A. Helene
1969 Tonque: One Pueblo's Glaze Pottery Industry Dominated Middle Rio Grande Commence. *El Palacio* 76: 36–42.
1981 A Petrographic Study of the Pottery of Gran Quivira. In "Contributions to Gran Quivira Archaeology," edited by Alden C. Hayes, pp. 67–74. *Publications in Archaeology* 17. National Park Service, Washington.

Warren, A. Helene, and Frances J. Mathien
1985 Prehistoric and Historic Turquoise Mining in the Cerrillos District: Time and Place. In "Southwestern Culture History: Collected Papers in Honor of Albert H. Schroeder," edited by Charles L. Lange, pp. 93–127. *Papers of the Archaeological Society of New Mexico* 10. Ancient City Press, Santa Fe.

Warren, A. Helene, and Robert H. Weber
1979 Indian and Spanish Mining in the Galisteo and Hagan Basins. In "Archaeology and History of Santa Fe County," edited by Raymond V. Ingersoll, pp. 7–11. *New Mexico Geological Society Special Publication* 8. Albuquerque.

Watson, Patty Jo, Steven A. LeBlanc, and Charles L. Redman
1980 Aspects of Zuni Prehistory: Preliminary Report on Excavations and Survey in the El Morro Valley of New Mexico. *Journal of Field Archaeology* 7: 201–218.

Weigand, Phil C.
1975 Aboriginal West Mexican Glazes and Their Possible Relationship to the Southwest. *Pottery Southwest* 2(2): 5–6.

Wenger, Etienne
1998 *Communities of Practice: Learning, Meaning, and Identity.* Cambridge University Press, Cambridge.

Western Mineral Products Company
n.d. The Property of the Western Mineral Products Company, Carthage, New Mexico. Manuscript, unpublished and undated report on file at the New Mexico Bureau of Mines and Mineral Resources, Socorro.

Whiteley, Peter
1988 *Deliberate Acts: Changing Hopi Culture Through the Oraibi Split.* University of Arizona Press, Tucson.

Wiessner, Polly
1983 Style and Social Information in Kalahari San Projectile Points. *American Antiquity* 48(2): 253–276.
1984 Reconsidering the Behavioral Basis for Style: A Case Study among the Kalahari San. *Journal of Anthropological Archaeology* 3(3): 190–234.
1985 Style or Isocrestic Variation? A Reply to Sackett. *American Antiquity* 50(1): 160–166.
1990 Is There a Unity to Style? In *The Uses of Style in Archaeology*, edited by Margaret W. Conkey and Christine A. Hastorf, pp. 105–112. Cambridge University Press, Cambridge.

Wilcox, David R.
1981 Changing Perspectives on the Protohistoric Pueblos, A.D. 1450–1700. In "The Protohistoric Period in the American Southwest, A.D. 1450–1700," edited by David R. Wilcox and W. Bruce Masse, pp. 378–409. *Arizona State University Anthropological Research Papers* 24. Arizona State University, Tempe.
1991 Changing Contexts of Pueblo Adaptations, A.D. 1200–1600. In *Farmers, Hunters, and Colonists: Interaction Between the Southwest and the Southern Plains*, edited by Katherine A. Spielmann, pp. 128–154. University of Arizona Press, Tucson.

Wilcox, David R., and Jonathan Haas
1994 The Scream of the Butterfly: Competition and Conflict in the Prehistoric Southwest. In *Themes in Southwestern Prehistory*, edited by George J. Gumerman, pp. 87–108. School of American Research Press, Santa Fe.

Wilcox, David R., G. Robertson, and J. S. Wood
2000 Perry Mesa, a 14th Century Gated Community in Central Arizona. *Plateau Journal* 10: 45–61.

Wills, Wirt H., and Robert D. Leonard
1994 Preface. In *The Ancient Southwestern Community*, edited by Wirt H. Wills and Robert D. Leonard, pp. xiii–xvi. University of New Mexico Press, Albuquerque.

Wilson, C. A., J. R. Bacon, M. S. Cresser,
and D. A. Davidson
  2006   Lead Isotope Ratios as a Means of Sourcing
         Anthropogenic Lead in Archaeological Soils: A
         Pilot Study of an Abandoned Shetland Croft.
         Archaeometry 48(3): 501–509.
Wobst, H. Martin
  1977   Stylistic Behavior and Information Exchange.
         In *For the Director: Research Essays in Honor
         of James B Griffin*, edited by Charles E.
         Cleland, pp. 317–342. University of Michigan,
         Museum of Anthropology, Ann Arbor.
Wolf, S., S. Stos, R. Mason,
and M. S. Tite
  2003   Lead Isotope Analyses of Islamic Pottery
         Glazes from Fustat, Egypt. *Archaeometry* 45(3):
         405– 420.
Woodbury, Richard B., and Nathalie F. S. Woodbury
  1956   Zuni Prehistory and El Morro National Monu-
         ment. *Southwestern Lore* 21: 56–60.
  1966   Decorated Pottery of the Zuni Area. In "The
         Excavation of Hawikuh by Frederick Webb
         Hodge: Report of the Hendricks-Hodge Expedi-
         tion," by Watson Smith, Richard B. Woodbury,

and Nathalie F. S. Woodbury, pp. 302–336.
*Contributions from the Museum of the Ameri-
can Indian, Heye Foundation* 20. Museum of
the American Indian, New York.
Wright, R. P.
  1984   Technology and Style in Ancient Ceramics. In
         Ceramics and Civilization, Vol. 1: *Ancient
         Technology to Modern Science*, edited by
         William D. Kingery, pp. 5–25. The American
         Ceramic Society, Columbus, Ohio.
Zedeño, María Nieves
  1994   Sourcing Prehistoric Ceramics at Chodistaas
         Pueblo, Arizona: The Circulation of People and
         Pots in the Grasshopper Region. *Anthropologi-
         cal Papers of the University of Arizona* 58.
         University of Arizona Press, Tucson.
  1998   Defining Material Correlates for Ceramic
         Circulation in the Prehistoric Puebloan South-
         west. *Journal of Anthropological Research* 54:
         461–475.
Zier, Christian J.
  1976   Excavations Near Zuni, New Mexico: 1973.
         *Museum of Northern Arizona Research Paper
         2*. Museum of Northern Arizona, Flagstaff.

Index

Abstract

The Pueblo IV period (A.D. 1275–1600) witnessed dramatic changes in regional settlement patterns and social configurations across the ancestral Pueblo Southwest. Some areas were abandoned during this interval, but populations elsewhere consolidated into apartment-like nucleated pueblos. Early in the Pueblo IV period, ancestral Pueblo groups began making distinctive polychrome pottery vessels, often decorated with glaze paints, that have been linked with the introduction of new ideologies and religious practices to the area. Polychrome bowls likely were used not only for everyday household food service, but also as containers for ritual offerings and for serving food at community-wide feasts.

This research explores scales of interaction among residents of nucleated pueblo clusters in the Zuni region of west-central New Mexico during the thirteenth and fourteenth centuries A.D. by analyzing the production and exchange of polychrome and utility ware vessels, glaze paint recipes, use of color on polychrome pottery, and glaze paint ore sources. The ceramic sample comes from collections made previously at nine nucleated pueblos occupied during all or part of the A.D. 1275–1400 interval. Multiple lines of evidence, including INAA, electron microprobe, and lead isotope analyses, indicate that potters and those with access to their products used pottery to negotiate relationships at multiple scales: within pueblo clusters (local interaction spheres), among pueblo clusters (regional alliances), and with other regions.

Building on previous research, this study demonstrates that pueblos in different parts of the Zuni region consistently used locally available clay resources to make polychrome and utility ware vessels. Utility ware was sometimes exchanged at the level of the individual pueblo or pueblo cluster. Decorated bowls, however, were more frequently exchanged throughout the region, and the direction of this exchange was markedly from west to east. Pueblos in the El Morro Valley in the eastern Zuni region were the recipients of polychrome bowls from other parts of the Zuni region, a pattern interpreted as the result of interpueblo alliance formation within the context of integrative rituals hosted at El Morro Valley pueblos. There is also evidence for a relatively rapid, region-wide shift from a high copper/

Resumen

El período Pueblo IV (1275–1600 d.C.) marca unos cambios dramáticos en los patrones de asentamiento regionales y configuraciones sociales a través del suroeste norteamericano ancestral. Algunas áreas fueron abandonadas durante este intervalo, pero poblaciones en otros lugares se consolidaron en asentamientos altamenta nucleados. En el período Pueblo IV temprano, los grupos Pueblo empezaron la manufactura de distintivas vasijas polícromas, usualmente decoradas con pinturas vidriadas, las cuales han sido relacionadas con la introducción de nuevas ideologías y prácticas religiosas en esta área. Los cuencos polícromos fueron utilizados tanto en contextos domésticos como en rituales que requirieron ofrendas y servicio de comestibles en fiestas comunales.

Esta investigación explora las escalas de interacción entre residents de grupos de pueblos nucleados en la región Zuni al centro-oeste de Nuevo México durante los siglos XIII y XIV de esta era, por medio del análisis de la producción e intercambio de vasijas corriente y polícromas, recetas de pinturas vidriadas, uso del color, y fuentes de materia prima para pintura vidriada. La muestra cerámica proviene de colecciones previamente obtenidas en nueve pueblos nucleados ocupados durante todo o parte del intervalo 1275–1400 d.C. Múltiples líneas de evidencia, incluyendo INAA, microprobe electrónico, y análisis de isótopos de plomo, indican que los alfareros y aquéllos quienes tuvieron acceso a estos productos utilizaron cerámica para negociar relaciones a escalas multiples: dentro de cada pueblo (esferas de interacción local), así como entre varios pueblos (alianzas regionales) y con otras regiones.

Este estudio expande previas investigaciones y demuestra que los pueblos en diferentes partes de la región Zuni usaron consistentemente fuentes locales de arcilla para elaborar vasijas corriente y polícromas. Las vasijas corriente a veces fueron intercambiadas a nivel de pueblo o grupo de pueblos. Sin embargo, los cuencos decorados fueron frecuentemente intercambiados a través de la región, con una dirección marcadamente oeste-este. Los pueblos en el Valle del Morro recibieron cuencos polícromos de otras partes de la region Zuni—un patrón interpretado como el resultado de la formación de una alianza interpueblo